MoneySkills

101 Activities to Teach Your Child About Money

By Bonnie Drew

THE CAREER PRESS
180 FIFTH AVE.,
PO BOX 34
HAWTHORNE, NJ 07507
1-800-CAREER-1
201-427-0229 (OUTSIDE U.S.)
FAX: 201-427-2037

MONEYSKILLS: 101 ACTIVITIES TO TEACH YOUR CHILD ABOUT MONEY

ISBN 1-56414-011-3, $9.95

Cover design by Dean Johnson Design, Inc.

Copies of this book may be ordered by mail or phone directly from the publisher. To order by mail, please include price as noted above, $2.50 handling per order, plus $1.00 for each book ordered. (New Jersey residents please add 7% sales tax.) Send to: The Career Press Inc., 180 Fifth Avenue., PO Box 34, Hawthorne, NJ 07507.

Or call Toll-Free 1-800-CAREER-1 to order using your VISA or Mastercard or for further information on all titles published or distributed by Career Press.

The author and publisher are not liable for any accidents or injuries incurred due to the use or misuse of the activities suggested in this book. All activities, games, and projects should be conducted under supervision of a responsible adult.

Attention: Schools, Organizations, Corporations

This book is available at quantity discounts for bulk purchases for educational, business or sales promotional use. Please contact:
Gretchen Fry, Career Press, 180 Fifth Avenue
Hawthorne, NJ 07507
or call 1-800-CAREER-1

Contents

Dedication

To my family and special friends who have supported me through the many months of research, writing, and creating of this work. Thanks for your encouragement and the many sacrifices you made so that I could continue following my dream.

Chapter 1

Teaching Your Child the Financial Facts of Life

If you could be a fairy godmother and bestow one special gift of "Wisdom about Money" upon your child. . . what would you give?

What parents want kids to learn about money

Have you ever tried to sit down and make a list of all the basic facts about money your child should know before he turns 18? Don't feel guilty if you haven't. There are at least two good reasons why. First, like all parents, you're extremely busy. Second, teaching kids about money is not easy!

Money is a complex subject. And it's often complicated by long-observed family traditions, old habits, unpredictable income, unexpected expenses, and strong emotions. As a result, most parents aren't sure how to answer the question: *What do you want your child to learn about money?* The most common answer is, "More than anything else, I want my child to learn responsibility with money."

I like that, but what is this quality you call *responsibility,* and how can you tell when a child achieves the state of "being responsible?" Can you tell me how to *measure* responsibility?

Growing up responsible

Responsibility is not something we can pour into a box, tie with a pretty ribbon, and hand to our children. But wouldn't it be nice if we could? I picture it this way: Parents could go to this special place called The Valuable Trait Store. On the outside it doesn't look like much, but we'd go in anyway. And we'd walk up to the counter and look at all the valuable traits like Honesty, Integrity, Generosity, and Kindness all arranged attractively on the shelves. And we'd say, "I'd like to see what you have in Responsibility."

The clerk would say, "Well, we've got all kinds: Responsibility with Pets, Responsibility for Chores, Responsibility in Crossing Streets. And I need to know what size you want. Is this for you or your child?"

> Which of the following is RESPONSIBILITY?
>
> A. Not losing your lunch money on the way to school.
> B. Deciding to spend your money on stocks and bonds rather than bubblegum and candy.
> C. Not cheating on your income tax.
> D. None of the above.
> E. All of the above.

Ignoring the clerk's insinuation, we'd say "Show me Responsibility with Money for a child age 7." The clerk reaches way up on the top shelf and pulls down a box. We read the label. We study the ingredients. We open the box and look inside. It's just what we want. Responsibility with Money. "I'll take it. And can you gift wrap it for me?"

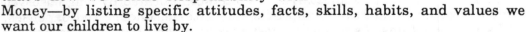

Then we'd hurry home and give it to our child. We'd feel so good, knowing we'd accomplished what many parents only dream of—imparting Responsibility with Money, guaranteeing our child will never make the mistakes we made, insuring him a future of financial stability.

Now I want to ask you—*what was in the box?* What attitudes, habits, and skills with money did you give your child? You see, that's how we define Responsibility with Money—by listing specific attitudes, facts, skills, habits, and values we want our children to live by.

"So what's the big deal?" you say. "Why do you keep asking me what I want my kid to know about money?"

Kids are consumers

Here's the big deal. Children have more money at their disposal today than in any previous generation. The Rand Youth Poll reveals that children influence more than a collective $150 billion spent by their families every year. A survey by Wendy's International, Inc. indicates that in 83 percent of American families, kids play the major role in deciding where the family eats out. In addition, 50 percent of the parents surveyed said that toy promotions affected their fast-food choices.

The Food Marketing Institute says children influence 78 percent of choices parents make on children's breakfast cereals and 72 percent of clothing choices. This survey also indicates that 65 percent of children go to the supermarket at least once a week, and children between the ages of 6 and 12 spend more than $7 billion a year. *That's* a big deal.

Dr. James U. McNeal, marketing professor at Texas A&M University has studied children's buying habits for more than 20 years. His most recent survey shows that a 10-year-old averages five purchases in five stores in a typical week. Dr. McNeal also found that girls under age 12 spend $10 million each year on cosmetics and toiletries. Furthermore, kids spend about $1 billion every Christmas.

If you don't think that's a big deal, retailers *do*. Big business knows children are consumers of great importance. That's why so many TV commercials, eye-catching store displays, and special promotions are all aimed at *your kids*. Smart retailers know that it's the kids who remember brand names and store names.

What does all this mean to you, as a parent? Kids spend a lot of their own money, and influence a majority of the choices *you* make with *your* money. Frankly, whether we like it or not, it's the kids who are calling most of the shots—and we'd better teach them to be good at it!

Who's teaching kids about money?

Here's another startling statistic: Surveys show that less than 40 percent of parents talk about money with their children. So where do kids learn money management? Not at school.

Margaret Welch, a certified financial planner in Washington, D.C., puts it bluntly: "With few exceptions, children learn almost nothing in school about financial realities that are of great importance to the average person. If a parent doesn't do the job, it doesn't get done." (*Family Circle*, Oct. 17, 1989, "Talking $$$ With Kids," Susan Jacoby).

Nancy McLaughlin, a consumer news reporter for the *Greensboro News & Record* recently told me a story that illustrates how ill-prepared most young people are to handle financial affairs. When Nancy was a freshman in college, she was at the bank one afternoon when she overheard another member of her class speaking to a customer service representative. The young man was very worried because his checkbook had been stolen. The customer service representative assured him that a stolen checkbook could be handled easily. The bank would watch the account closely and they would simply order him more checks starting with different numbers. Then the real problem was revealed. "You don't understand," exclaimed the young man, "In order to save time, I *signed all the checks!*" The shocked bank employee had no choice. She immediately closed the account.

If parents don't talk to kids about money and schools don't teach kids about money, a lot of young people are entering adulthood with almost no basic dollars-and-cents money management knowledge. The results are evident in our society: massive national debt, rampant consumer credit problems, and more individuals and businesses every year declaring bankruptcy.

Parents, our mission is clear: We *must* teach our children the financial facts of life! So let's get back to the question I asked earlier: What do you want your child to know about money? Use the *Financial Facts of Life* worksheet on the next page to set some specific goals for teaching your child about money.

Financial Facts of Life

1. Attitudes—What feelings or emotions about money do you want to pass along to the next generation? Example: generosity.

2. Values—What code of money ethics do you want your child to live by? Examples: honesty, family and health come before money.

3. Facts—What basic knowledge about money will be necessary for your child to function properly in society? Examples: How credit cards work; what savings bonds are.

4. Skills—What must your child be competent to do with money? Examples: making change, developing a weekly budget.

5. Habits—What regular financial practices should be a part of your child's life? Examples: saving, goal setting.

One step at a time

This book was written to help you reach your goals for teaching your child healthy attitudes, values, facts, skills, and habits with money. But kids don't learn all of this at once. They learn by taking one small step at a time. The 101 activities, games, and projects in this book are designed to teach age-appropriate lessons about money as your child becomes ready for each step.

- **The activities for ages 3 to 5 emphasize money *facts*.** Examples: A nickel is 5 cents; two nickels make a dime; we trade money for things we want to buy at the store.

- **The activities for ages 6 to 8 emphasize money *skills*.** Examples: Making change, estimating total costs, setting and reaching a one-month savings goal, and managing an allowance.

- **The activities for ages 9 to 12 emphasize forming desirable money *habits*—or becoming "money smart."** Examples: Learning to comparison shop, understanding how a checking account works, and taking initiative to earn extra money for special savings goals.

- **All of the activities teach money *attitudes* and money *values*.** But remember, kids get most of their money value system from watching parents.

Caution: Kids watch what parents *do*!

The research conducted by Dr. James McNeal of Texas A&M University shows that the way children manage money is mostly determined or influenced by parents' behavior with money. That means your *walk* has got to match your *talk*! Your kids watch what you do with money. Your own money habits are the examples your kids will follow. No matter what you say, kids get the message by what you *do*.

Before you start using the activities in this book, take some time to examine your own attitudes about money:

1. Is your approach to financial matters calm and rational?
2. Do you argue about money? Neglect savings? Live from paycheck to paycheck?
3. Do you feel guilty about money? Anxious? Afraid?
4. Do you need money to feel "good enough?"
5. Is money a way to express love, anger, guilt, power?
6. Do you overspend? Do you often buy on impulse?
7. Is shopping a pastime or a cure for depression?
8. Is money *the* goal, or a tool to meet goals?
9. Do you pay bills on time?
10. Do you believe in sharing with the less fortunate?

Look closely at your attitudes and behaviors with money. Money is often the way we express love, anger, guilt, power, status and self-esteem. Sometimes we use money as a weapon: "While you were home enjoying your nice air-conditioned house and TV, I was out working so you could eat and have clothes to wear." Or we use money to retaliate: "She spent all that money on clothes, so I'm going to buy myself that new drill I've been wanting." Many of us use money to create an image. We buy cars, clothes, a house—all symbols of success—to show we're *good enough*.

Today, a lot of parents substitute money or gifts for love. They feel bad about not being able to spend time with their kids, so they buy them something. The message of materialism comes across loud and clear.

Are we rich yet?

Let's be clear about what money is *not*. Money is not taboo, evil, or dirty. It is not something to be kept secret. Nor is it love, power, or a measure of personal worth. Money doesn't buy happiness. Children should never get the idea that the more money you have, the more worthy a person you are.

Instead, children should be taught to view money as purely a medium of exchange. Avoid materialism by stressing the importance of charity and sharing. Let your child know that family and health are more important than money.

A few years ago, a mother wrote to Ann Landers for advice because her 12-year-old wanted to know, "Are we rich?" Ann Landers answered that a person is rich if he has good health, a loving family, and peace with himself. That's the attitude we need to get across to this generation! Money is simply a medium of exchange to get things we need to live. True wealth is good health, a loving family, and peace within ourselves.

"A hug, a smile, a kiss or time spent together is something money can't buy. And that may be the most important money lesson of all."

Marie Hodge
(*Readers Digest*, Jan., 1989,
"Teach Your Kids About Money")

How children learn best

Although it is vitally important that parents set a good example about money, that alone is not enough. Parents must teach their children a body of basic financial knowledge—facts and skills that will stay with them forever.

With children under 12, it is not a matter of sitting down and talking about the family finances. Children learn by doing touching, counting, playing, and experimenting—actively experiencing the world around them. That's why **MoneySkills** provides 101 *activities*, not 101 lectures! When we involve kids in hands-on learning activity, they remember.

Each activity in MoneySkills is included based on four criteria:

1. The activity has solid educational value.

2. The activity is easy, inexpensive, and fun for kids and parents. (It's "user-friendly.")
3. The activity goes along with daily routines. (It's "everyday.")
4. The activity can be changed, adapted, and used over and over as the child progresses.

MoneySkills is not a program that makes parents into martyrs or slaves who race from activity to activity, feeling guilty because they can't get it all done. Instead I invite parents to use this book as a resource guide. Start anywhere, browse through, pick what you like, make changes for different situations, take something out, add something, combine several activities, or even invent new ones.

Children learn at different rates

Nothing is wrong with your child if he is 6 years old but he's not ready for the activities in the chapter for ages 6-8. Not every activity recommended for a particular age group will be appropriate for your child because "the book says so." Children grow and develop and get ready to learn at different rates.

As you browse through the following chapters, you will find some activities that are obviously at challenge-level for your child. These activities are for children whose parents have been teaching them about money for a period of time. Ideally parents would get this book and start teaching their child about money when he or she is 3. If parents use this book faithfully and help their child accomplish the appropriate learning goals for each age, that child most likely will be able to accomplish even the most challenging activities in each chapter.

Learning about money is fun!

Don't feel that it's necessary to force your child to engage in the activities in this book. All children are naturally curious about what goes on around them. When your child asks questions or expresses interest in what you are doing with money, it's the natural time to suggest a game or an activity from *MoneySkills*.

Most important, make learning fun. Sharla Feldscher, author of *The Kidfun Activity Book*, says you can teach kids anything if they are having fun. She's right! So relax and look forward to happy memories of fun and sharing, special conversations, and routine family activities turned into exciting learning experiences. Let learning by playful, joyous, and part of your daily life.

Be prepared: This is a long-term project

Teaching your child about money is an ongoing effort. It starts the day you first help your child put a penny in the gum machine and continues even beyond the day you help him move into his first apartment.

It's up to parents to create a healthy learning environment for their children's financial education. So be prepared to let your child make some mistakes along the way. Be prepared to *listen* rather than lecture. Be prepared to answer tough questions honestly. And be prepared for some good laughs, because above all else, learning about money together is an adventure you'll remember forever.

How to create a healthy environment for learning about money

1. Most important, treat children with dignity and help them feel good about themselves.
2. Teach your children the joy of learning. Initiate activities by "suggesting" rather than commanding.
3. Listen and communicate with your kids. Avoid criticism or any hint of ridicule. If you show anger or make your children feel stupid, you will discourage them from trying again.
4. Let kids learn more from experience than from lectures. Ask questions and encourage them to find answers, but give them the freedom to make choices.
5. When you give your children opportunities to make choices, follow their decisions without question. Your children learn to make better choices when they are able to see the natural consequences of their decisions.
6. Avoid comparing your children to other kids, or even worse, yourself at that age.
7. Expect kids to make some mistakes. Be patient and avoid saying "I told you so!" They need your moral support when things go wrong.
8. Money management is only one *part* of raising children. Treat it seriously, but don't over-emphasize money and materialism.
9. Expect kids to do as you do, not as you *say*.
10. Remember that love and attention are the best learning aids a parent can use.

Tell me, I forget.
  Show me, I remember.
    Involve me, I understand.
      (Chinese proverb)

Chapter 2

MoneySkills for Ages 3 to 5

The curiosity of a 3-year-old is almost impossible to satisfy. A 3-year-old, in fact, has one favorite word: WHY? Why is the grass green? Why do you have to go to work? Why do toes wiggle? Why doesn't Kitty like it when I throw her in the bathtub? Why is it raining today? Why do you want to rest now?

Play is the way a child learns

Play is a very effective tool for teaching your child about money—play is the way children learn. For children, play is not a frivolous activity for when you have nothing better to do. Play is the way children try out new skills, explore the world, express feelings, satisfy curiosity, and practice to be "grown up."

When you introduce an activity from *MoneySkills*, suggest to your child, "Let's play a game." That won't be hard, because most of the activities in this chapter involve games of memory, matching, guessing, make-believe, pretending, making something, or finding things.

One good way to get children interested is to simply start playing the game yourself. Gather the materials for a *MoneySkills* activity you think your child will enjoy. Then just sit down and start making it, playing with it, drawing it, or building it. Your child will soon be at your side asking questions and wanting to help.

Special ideas to make games and activities fun

- Pretend you are spies looking for clues to a mystery.
- Speak in a whisper, a high voice, a low voice.
- Talk with a heavy French accent or a slow Western drawl.
- Send mysterious "secret" messages.
- Ask questions that make your child curious.
- Ask your child to be the "judge" who must pick a winner or time an activity.
- Be an elephant, an ant, a giant, an astronaut.
- Be a typewriter, a washing machine, a living scale.
- Play the game blindfolded.

- Play the game with one hand behind your back.
- Pretend you are on a magic carpet.
- Invite a favorite doll or teddy bear to play.
- Drape a sheet over a table to make a special hideout.
- Have a race.
- Instead of walking, skip or hop.
- Use kitchen tongs to pick up things and put them away.
- Take inside games outside.

Guidelines for using *MoneySkills* activities with preschoolers

- Avoid pushing your child into activities he is not ready for. Introduce *MoneySkills* activities as your child seems ready.
- Your child loves to be part of what you do. Allow him to join you in activities.
- Avoid too much structure, thus turning play into work.
- Take into consideration a child's short attention span. Stop when your child becomes disinterested, frustrated, or inattentive. Try the activity again some other time.
- Alter the activity as necessary to meet the needs of your child.
- Don't expect preschoolers to understand abstract concepts.
- Encourage open communication by getting down on your child's level. Eye contact is very important.
- Remember that your child may not understand all the words you say, but he does understand your facial expression and the tone of your voice.
- When your child has difficulty with an activity, praise him for his effort and what he did accomplish. Show no displeasure about what he failed to do, even if he did it right yesterday.
- Repeat activities or use a similar activity within a week to reinforce what the child learned the first time.

Your child's first experiences with money

Whether you are aware of it, your child has probably already learned a great deal more than you think about money. When did that happen? Every time you took your child with you to the grocery store!

Small children absorb a wide variety of messages as they observe how parents handle money. They notice the expression on your face, the tone of your voice, how you feel about shopping, what kinds of things you put in your basket, how carefully you consider buying decisions, and how you exchange money for the things you want to buy.

Your child knows a lot about "shopping behavior" already! Remember that children learn by copying your actions. If you always pay for things with a credit card, they see that little piece of plastic as "magic money." If you look for things on sale, they learn to be bargain hunters. Take advantage of your time together in the grocery store to give your child "mini-lessons" about money.

Ways to involve your pre-schooler in shopping

1. As you shop, take time to explain what you are looking for and how you make buying decisions. Your child may not understand everything you say, but she will remember the importance you place on being a smart shopper.

2. Make a game of looking for pictures on packages and identifying products the family uses. "On this aisle we are going to buy graham crackers. See if you can find the box with the picture of graham crackers on the front."

3. Encourage your child to name things she sees in the store. Show her new kinds of fruit and vegetables. Let her touch and smell.

4. Ask your child to help count things as you put them in a bag or in the cart.

5. Involve your child in making choices. "Shall we buy green grapes or purple grapes today?" Explain that we can't buy everything, so we decide what we want or need the most.

6. Show your child how you trade your money for the things you are buying.

Practice making choices and trading

As you shop together, there will be many opportunities to teach your child about trading and making choices. "Shall we choose the red ball or the blue ball for Angela's birthday party?" "Do you want popcorn or pretzels for snack time?" "We only have enough money to buy one T-shirt. Do you like the one with the bear or the one with the monkey?"

Even stopping for gas or refreshments at the corner convenience store can be a learning experience:

1. Give your child enough money to buy a small carton of juice.

2. Show your child that she can choose from orange juice, apple juice, or grape juice.

3. Explain that her money is enough to buy only one carton of juice. Show her the price tag.

4. Let her choose the juice and take it to the checkout counter.

5. Explain that when we give the storekeeper the money for the juice, the juice is ours. The store keeps our money and we keep the juice. We like to trade our money for things we want!

Shopping problems

Every parent dreads the embarrassment of having a screaming child throw a fit in the middle of the grocery store. I don't guarantee you'll never, *ever* have to deal with a screaming toddler, but a set of ground rules put into practice at an early age will prevent many bad habits.

Ground rules for shopping

1. Remember the old warning about never shopping hungry. Take along a healthy snack for your child to eat while in the store if necessary.

2. Be clear about your shopping mission for the day. "Today we're shopping to buy good food for the family to eat (not to buy toys)."
3. Realize that displays in stores are meant to attract kids. However, you should never reward a child who begs for something by buying it. Establish a rule from the very beginning that people who beg or misbehave get nothing.
4. Reward appropriate behavior with hugs, words of appreciation, or letting your child choose something special when you are ready to check out. "I liked the way you stayed beside me in the store today. Why don't we buy some gum to chew on the way home?"

You may want to add additional rules of your own to this list. It's most important to adhere to your ground rules each and every time you take your child shopping—even on days when you are stressed, tired, worried about your child, or in a hurry. Children learn to go by the rules when parents are consistent.

Avoiding hassle is not the only reason to establish ground rules for shopping. Look again. These rules teach patience, politeness, respect for others, and self-discipline. And even more important, your child is learning to delay gratification, and to have a plan for the way you spend your money. We'll be working more on these skills in the activities that follow.

Activities That Teach Money *Facts*

A child's first lessons about money

Three-year-olds are busy learning about their world! And in order to understand the world today, a child must understand money. Age 3, then, is the natural time to start a child's first lessons about money.

Preschoolers need basic money facts. Your child will be ready to learn what money is (coins and paper bills) and what it does (you buy things with it). At age 3, we concentrate on concrete facts, not abstract ideas. Your child is not ready to discuss "saving for college," but she is ready to touch, count, name the coins, and explore what money is all about.

By age 5, your child will be ready to start managing a small allowance and be able to grasp beginning concepts about responsibility with money. The following list is an overview of the money facts your child will learn with the activities in this chapter.

What to teach children ages 3 to 5 about money
Age 3:
- To identify coins by their correct names
- To identify dollar bills

- To keep money in a safe place
- How to trade coins for something when you go shopping

Age 4:
- To know how many cents each coin is worth
- To count cents with a few coins at a time
- When we spend money, it is gone
- We can't buy everything, so we make choices

Age 5:
- To know basic coin equivalents
- To match small amounts of money with things that are affordable
- To start managing a small allowance
- To know where money comes from (usually work)
- Banks help keep our money safe until we need it
- Writing a check takes our money out of the bank

1. My Very Own Toy Store!

In just a few minutes you can turn a corner of your child's room into her Very Own Toy Store. Then let your child practice what she's learned while shopping with you.

How to set up

1. Arrange some of your child's favorite toys on a table or shelf.
2. Use colored dots from the office supply store to make price tags your child can read. For example: Two dots means the price is two coins, tokens, or play dollars.
3. Supply additional props to make the game more fun: A purse or wallet to carry "money," shopping bags from favorite stores, a play cash register.

How the game works

Suggest that your child pretend she is going shopping, arriving at the store, looking at everything, choosing a toy to buy. Let her try out the toys and pick her favorite. Show your child how to exchange play money or real money from her bank for a toy. The child pays the same number of coins or tokens as there are dots on the tag. Then let her put the toy in a shopping bag and pretend to take it home.

For more fun

Pretend to dress up to go shopping, drive a car, take a baby along, or shop for a birthday present. Your child will love creating her own stories to act out.

For more challenge

Make the decisions a little harder by giving your child a budget for her pretend shopping excursion. Give her a few more tokens, so that she can choose more than one item to buy. This will encourage her to make decisions. Should she buy the big teddy bear and the story book? Or would she rather have the red car and the rubber duck?

MoneySkills

✔We trade money for things we want to buy.
✔We can't buy everything, so we choose what we like the best.

---

2. Coin Cards

A child who has been involved in shopping and understands that we trade money for things we want to buy is ready to learn about our currency. The card games in this activity make it fun to learn the names of our coins. You will need two sets of cards.

Three ways to make coin flash cards

1. Photocopy the following sample flash cards on card stock or heavy paper (see page 20).
2. From the photocopies, make two sets of 3 X 5 cards—so you'll have two penny cards, two nickel cards, two dime cards and two quarter cards.
3. Tape real coins to 3 x 5 cards.

Let the games begin!

Show your child the four matching sets of cards. Discuss ways the coins in each set are the same. Then show your child ways the coins are different from each other. Use the names of the coins over and over as you talk. Now play some matching games.

Game 1

Lay one card from each set out in a row face up. Shuffle and stack the remaining four cards face down. Let your child draw a card from the stack and find the one that is the same. Use the words "the same" over and over.

Game 2

Play a game of concentration. Turn all of the cards face down. Then show your child how to turn two cards over at a time, searching for cards that are "the same." If the pictures don't match, say "those are not the same." Turn them over and keep playing until the matches are found.

For very young children

- Say the names of the coins as often as possible as you play.
- Remember your child's short attention span. When your child shows signs of restlessness, it's time to stop for now.
- To end the game, turn all the cards face up. Let your child help you match all the cards so you can put them away.
- Encourage your child to choose a special place to keep the cards so you can continue the game another time.

MoneySkills
✔Coins can be recognized by their markings.
✔Coins have names.

Your child needs a safe place to keep money. If your child doesn't have a piggy bank, this is a good time to make one. Use a clear plastic margarine or whipped topping bowl. Cut a slit in the lid large enough to drop coins through. Let your child decorate by gluing on pictures, play money, pieces of yarn, bits of ribbon, or drawing a design with markers.

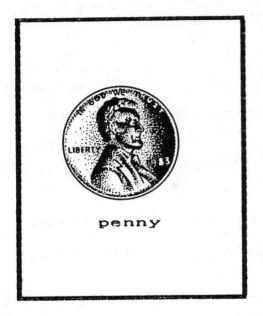

penny

nickel

dime

quarter

3. What is a Penny?

Children like to learn things by hearing stories! To help your child tell the difference between a penny, nickel, dime and quarter, tell him short "stories" about the famous people pictured on the faces of our coins.

Learning about pennies

Show your child a penny. Talk about what it looks like: its copper color, smooth edges, Lincoln's picture. "Do you see the man's face on the penny? That is a picture of Abraham Lincoln. He was a famous man and was once the president of the United States." Tell your child anything you may remember about Abraham Lincoln, but keep it short.

Then turn the coin over and show him the building on the other side. "This is a picture of the Lincoln Memorial. This building was named in honor of President Abraham Lincoln." Explain that this coin is called a penny.

What do we do with pennies?

We can buy things at the store with pennies. But we need a safe place to keep money until we go to the store. "Let's put the pennies in your bank."

Learning about nickels

Use this same activity another day to show your child a nickel. Talk about how we can recognize a nickel: its silver color, the picture of President Thomas Jefferson, and the picture of his home, Monticello, on the back of the coin. "What do we do with a nickel?" We keep nickels safe in our bank until we go to the store. Let your child put some nickels in his bank.

United States Coins

Coin	Face	Reverse
Penny	Abraham Lincoln	Lincoln Memorial
Nickel	Thomas Jefferson	Monticello
Dime	Franklin D. Roosevelt	Torch & olive branch
Quarter	George Washington	American Eagle
Half-dollar	John F. Kennedy	Great Seal of the U.S.

Learning about dimes and quarters

When your child has become very familiar with pennies and nickels and has played some of the sorting and matching games in the activities that follow, she will be ready to learn the stories of our dime and quarter.

Point out to your child the smaller size of the dime, its rough edges, the picture of yet another president, Franklin Roosevelt, and the torch and olive branch on the back that stand for our country's desire for peace.

When you and your child study the quarter, let her notice its larger size, the picture of the eagle on the back and George Washington on the front. You can tell her the story of the cherry tree and why he is called "the father of our country."

For further reinforcement

Repeat often the stories you discuss about the coins. Soon your child will be able to "help" you tell the story. Then really applaud her when she is able to tell the story herself!

MoneySkills
✔We recognize coins by their color, size, shape, and markings.
✔We keep money in a safe place.

---

4. Let's Fish!

This game is much like the one your child loves at the school carnival. Use it to give your child practice calling coins by their correct names.

How to make fish

Cut four fish shapes from construction paper. Let your child draw eyes and a mouth for the fish. Then tape a coin to each one: penny, nickel, dime, quarter. Or paste a picture of each coin on the fish.

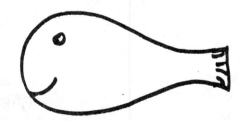

How to play fish

1. Start the game by asking your child to pretend that a table or certain area on the floor is the water. Show him the fish and name the coin on each one.
2. Now tell him to put the fish in the water. (He lays the fish out on the table or floor.)
3. Now tell him to pick up the fish with a penny on its back. Praise him if he is correct. Show him the right one if he doesn't know yet.

4. Continue "catching fish" and putting them in a bucket or trash can (your pretend fish pail). When all the fish are caught, dump them out and start over.

5. On another day, glue or tape a paper clip to the mouth of each fish. Tie a refrigerator magnet or cup hook magnet to a string. Show your child how to "catch" the fish with the magnet. Say the names of the coins over and over as you play the game.

For a challenge

1. Add a second set of fish to the game. "Now find two fish with pennies on their backs."

2. Color-code the fish and say, "See if you can catch a red fish with a nickel on its back."

MoneySkills

✔We can recognize pennies, nickels, dimes, and quarters by their size and special markings.

✔We can call the coins by their names.

---

5. A Penny is One Cent

Preschoolers have a hard time understanding the value of our coins. It is even more confusing when pennies are different colors, and dimes are smaller than nickels but worth more cents. Here are some ways to help your child start making sense out of cents values.

New pennies and old pennies

Get 10 new pennies and 10 old pennies from the bank. Look at the pennies with your child. Explain that some pennies are bright because they are new. As pennies are used over and over to buy things and lots of people handle them, they turn dull brown. Show your child that Lincoln's head is on all the coins.

Now dump all the pennies into a bowl. Let your child practice sorting the 10 new pennies into one cup and the 10 old pennies into another cup.

Paper pennies

Let your child make pretend pennies from brown paper. Use a penny to trace the round circles and write "1 cent" in each circle. (You may need to cut the circles out for very young children.) As you work together, sing this song:

(Tune: "The Farmer in the Dell")

A penny is one cent.

A penny is one cent.

I love to count and know,

A penny is one cent.

To make your paper pennies last longer, glue them to cardboard or posterboard circles. Save your pretend pennies to use as play money in other activities.

Counting pennies

Label egg carton sections with numbers 1 through 12. Show your child how to count the corresponding number of pennies into each section. How many cents are in each section?

Now pour the pennies out of the egg carton and let your child see if he can do it again by himself.

MoneySkills

✔Some pennies are bright copper and some are dull brown, but they all have the picture of Lincoln.

✔A penny is worth one cent.

---

6. A Pretend Supermarket

Preschoolers love to practice counting money and buying things in their own pretend supermarket!

Involve your child in creating the store

1. Find a place for your pretend supermarket: the corner of a room, or basement.

2. Save things from the kitchen to stock the store shelves. Use clean, empty containers from products your child recognizes: pudding cups, cereal boxes, peanut butter jars, catsup bottles, and egg cartons.

3. Make a cash drawer by inserting cardboard to make compartments in a plastic school box with a lid.
4. Supply the store with grocery bags and paper to make receipts—perhaps an old roll of calculator paper.
5. Use a play grocery cart, wagon, or basket for the grocery cart. Continue adding products, signs and props to the store as time goes on.

How to operate your store

Take turns being the customer and the storekeeper. Make sure you have play money or tokens for the customer to carry and for the storekeeper to put in the cash drawer.

When your child is learning about pennies, label the groceries with price tags that say 1 cent, 2 cents, etc. Let her use real pennies to buy things. As your child learns to count nickels, let her practice buying things that cost 5 cents, 10 cents (5 cents + 5 cents), etc. Each time your child takes a new step in learning to count money, adjust the supermarket pricing system to give practice with new skills.

Extra challenges

1. Introduce coin combinations by pricing items: 6 cents (5 cents + 1 cent), 16 cents (10 + 5 + 1), etc.
2. Let older children practice adding actual amounts and making change. Make the prices realistic, but easy to add.

MoneySkills
✔We can trade money for things we want.
✔We count our money and pay the storekeeper for what we buy.

---

7. Digging for Treasure

Children are fascinated with the idea of digging for buried treasure! This play-and-learn activity is a great way to get kids to practice recognizing and naming coins.

How to set up

Fill a box or dishpan with sand, rice, beans, clean kitty litter, or packing peanuts. Spread an old shower curtain or a large garbage bag under the "treasure box" to catch spills. Or take this activity outdoors.

Hunting for treasure

1. Hide five pennies in the box of sand. Let your child pretend to dig for treasure.
2. After he finds the pennies, hide five nickels in the sand. "Now what kind of treasure can you find in the box?"

3. Next, hide both the pennies and the nickels in the box. As your child finds the treasure, have him put the pennies in one pile and the nickels in another pile.
4. Ask him to count the pennies and nickels. "How many pennies did you find?" "How many nickels did you find?"
5. When your child learns to recognize other coins, add five dimes to the treasure hunt and then five quarters.

MoneySkills
✔We can identify, name, and match coins even when they are mixed up.
✔When we count coins, we are learning to count money.

---

8. Coin Rubbings and Embossings

Children love to make play money. This activity describes several ways to make play money with ordinary things you find around the house.

As you work together, talk about the details of each coin, its special markings, the man's face on the coin, the size, etc. Coin rubbings and embossings fascinate children and help them remember coins by identifying details about our coins.

Paper rubbings of nickels

Cut holes the size of nickels in a piece of posterboard. Put nickels in the holes and tape thin paper over the nickels. Then let your child rub a crayon over the paper until "nickels" appear. Cut out the rubbings and paste them to the round circles of posterboard you cut out earlier. Show your child how to write 5 cents on the back of each. Sing "A nickel is 5 cents" to the tune of "The Farmer in the Dell" (as in Activity 5).

Paper embossings of dimes

Here's how to make coin rubbings without actually marking on the paper. Place a dime under crisp paper. Use a firm object such as a cap from a ballpoint pen to rub over the coin. These embossed circles can be cut out, pasted on cardboard, and used for play money. Have your child write 10 cents on the back of each. As your child works, explain that a dime is worth 10 cents. Sing "A dime is worth 10 cents."

Foil embossings of quarters

Cover a quarter with aluminum foil and rub until the design shows through. Then help your child cut out the "quarters" and paste them on cardboard. Instruct your child to write 25 cents on the back of each. Sing "A quarter is 25 cents."

For additional enhancement

Give your child a chance to "spend" some of his "money." Pretend your kitchen is a snack bar and let your child "buy" a snack for the two of you.

MoneySkills
✔We can recognize coins by their special color, size, shape and markings.
✔Each coin has its own cents value.

---

9. The Box Game

Games make it fun to learn! This activity shows how to turn ordinary cardboard boxes into a game that helps children remember the special markings on our coins.

How to get ready

1. When you go to the grocery store, bring home a large cardboard box in which a child could easily crawl.
2. Find two small boxes. Inside each small box, place one penny, one nickel, one dime, and one quarter.

How to play the game

1. Turn the large cardboard box on its side and place one of the small boxes you prepared in its corner.
2. Give your child the other small box. Ask her to open the box and examine the coins.
3. Then tell her to choose one coin, say its name, look at it very closely, and lay it down on the table.
4. She should then crawl into the large box, sit down, and find the matching coin from the small box you placed there.
5. When she finds the right coin, she should crawl back out of the box and bring the coin to the table.
6. The matched coins should be placed side by side on a table and the steps above repeated until all the coins have been matched.

For a special surprise

Place a button or checker piece with the coins. Then ask, "What doesn't belong in the box today?" How is the button like a coin? (It's round.) How is it different? (It's not money.)

MoneySkills

✔We match pennies, nickels, dimes, and quarters by remembering and matching their size and special markings.

✔Other objects may be the same size and shape at coins, but they are not money.

---

10. Sorting Coins: Heads or Tails?

Preschoolers need practice recognizing coins when they are all mixed together. Try these sorting games.

A simple way to get started

1. Put five pennies, five nickels, and two cups on the table. Sit with your child and show him the coins.
2. Now mix the pennies and nickels. Ask him to pick up all the pennies and put them in one of the cups.

3. Now have him pour the pennies out and mix them with the nickels again. Ask him to find all the nickels and put them in a cup.

4. Then have him mix all the coins together again. This time, let him sort the pennies in one cup and the nickels in the other cup.

Muffin pan sorting

Put a dime in a bowl of pennies, nickels, and buttons. Ask your child to find the dime. Or set a bowl of assorted coins, washers, and buttons on the table. Let your child separate the items from the bowl into sections of a muffin pan. How many dimes did you find? How many quarters?

Fun with heads & tails

1. Explain that the side of the coin with the man's head is called "heads." The other side is called "tails."

2. Dump the cup of pennies on the table. Which ones landed on heads? Which ones landed on tails? Dump the nickels and see how they land. Put the coins back in the cups, dump them again. Did you get the same number of heads and tails?

3. Show your child how to spin a nickel and roll a nickel. How did it land? Heads or tails?

4. Now let him balance a nickel on the tip of his finger and see how far he can walk across the room. When the coin falls, does it land on heads or tails?

MoneySkills

✔ We recognize coins by their color, size, and markings even when they are mixed up.

✔ The face of a coin is called "heads" and the back is called "tails."

---

11. What's Missing?

Guessing games are a great way to help your child review what she knows about money. Use praise generously as you play!

Here's what to do

1. Lay a penny, a nickel, a dime, and a quarter on the table. Have your child identify each coin as you give directions. "Touch the penny." "Now touch the quarter." Sing the cent song that goes with each coin.

2. Now tell your child to turn around. Take one of the coins away. "Okay, turn around now. Which coin is missing?" Praise her if she is right. If she isn't, show her the missing coin.

3. When your child's skill at this game has increased, make the game a little harder by also changing the position of the coins each time.

Use modeling dough for extra fun

1. Press soft modeling dough into a thick "pancake." Let your child press the face of a penny into the dough.

2. "Can you see Abraham Lincoln's face in the dough?" Review the story of Abraham Lincoln and why his face is on the penny.

3. Now press a nickel and a dime into the dough. Tell the stories about Thomas Jefferson and Franklin Roosevelt again.

4. Have your child hide her eyes. Press each coin firmly into the dough. Place the coins on the table and mix them up.

5. Ask your child to look at the coins and match them with the impressions in the dough. Surprise her with something different in the group: a button or a paper clip. "Which thing doesn't belong here?"

MoneySkills

✔ We know that a penny is 1 cent, a nickel is 5 cents, a dime is 10 cents, and a quarter is 25 cents.

✔ We identify and remember the names of coins by studying their size and special markings.

---

12. What is a Dollar Bill?

Children are curious about paper money. Your child will enjoy hearing the story of our dollar bill. Help him make pretend dollar bills to spend at a "toy store."

Talk about a dollar bill

Start out by showing your child a dollar bill. Talk about what it looks like, its color, the official numbers, and George Washington's picture. Tell a short story from things you remember about George Washington.

Fun with play dollar bills

1. Cut green construction paper into strips about the size of dollar bills. Let your child use a black crayon or felt tip pen to write "1" and other markings on the "dollar bills."
2. Make five pretend wallets by folding sheets of construction paper in half and taping them on the ends.
3. Label the wallets with numbers 1 to 5. Ask your child to count the corresponding number of dollar bills into each wallet.
4. Arrange toys, books, and games on a table or shelf. "Let's pretend to buy things with our play dollar bills!"
5. Label everything two ways: with the actual amount ($2), and with pictures of the amount (draw two dollar bills).
6. Help your child count the number of dollars in the picture, and then decide which wallet has enough money to pay for the toy. Have him count the dollar bills as he pays the "storekeeper."
7. Now tell your child to turn his back. Put different amounts of his play dollars in an old wallet or purse. Let him guess and then count how many dollars he has to spend at the "toy store."

For more fun

The next time you go to the store, find something that costs $1 and let your child pay for it with a real dollar bill.

MoneySkills

✔Some of our money is made of paper. We call these "dollar bills."

✔We know how much money we have by counting our dollar bills.

---

13. Giant Money

Act out a story about a great giant who is coming to your town for a visit. "The giant needs our help. He doesn't have any money to buy food or things he needs. Let's make some giant money for him to use while he is here!"

How to make giant money

Help your child cut large circles out of posterboard or paper plates. Make the circles various sizes to represent the coins. Cut large rectangles for dollar bills. Then let your child draw and color the giant money.

Invent stories about the giant

- Is this a hungry giant from outer space who wants to taste a real hamburger?
- Is this a child giant from another land who has never been to a toy store?

Your child may want to pretend to be the giant. Or several children can take turns being the giant while others "help" the giant learn how we use money.

The giant wants to see a movie!

Pretend you are at the movies by setting up a row of chairs and watching a favorite cartoon on TV. Make some popcorn and lemonade. Let the giant use his giant money to buy movie tickets and refreshments for everyone.

Make a poster with giant money

When the game is over, mount the giant coins and dollar bills on a sheet of posterboard. Help your child write the value beside each one. Then mount a sample of real money beside each. Display the poster in a place where your child will see it and review it often.

MoneySkills
- ✔Everyone has to have money to trade for things they want to buy.
- ✔Each coin and dollar bill has special markings that help us remember its proper name and value.

Activities That Increase Money *Skills*

As your child learns the basic money facts described in this chapter, you will also want to teach important money skills. Watch for opportunities to use everyday activities to show your child how we use money.

- Give your child money to buy something from a machine when you go to the store. Let him put the money in and learn to operate the machine.

- Show your older preschooler how to put a quarter in a pay phone and call home. (Make sure someone is home to answer, or call a favorite friend and let your child say hello.)
- Show your child how to put a quarter in the newspaper stand and buy today's paper.

Question: When is *nine* of something less than one?

Answer: When the nine are pennies and the one is a dime!

It's not hard to understand why it is difficult for young children to understand money!

When your child is comfortable with identifying coins and bills and has a fairly good understanding of the cents value of our coins and bills, he is ready to learn to make change. Children usually start learning to make change in kindergarten, but they need lots of practice and are not expected to master the skill until second grade.

The first step in learning to make change is understanding *simple* coin equivalents: One nickel equals five pennies; One dime equals two nickels or 10 pennies. When your child is in first grade, more advanced coin equivalents will be introduced.

Remember, even adults occasionally make mistakes counting change! Be patient. Use the activities that follow over and over. With time and a little growing up, your child will master these concepts.

14. Snack Crackers

Use common daily routines like snack time to help your child understand coin equivalents.

How much is 5 cents?

1. Place five pennies and one nickel on the table. How many pennies do we have? How many nickels do we have?
2. Talk about how much the coins are worth. "How much is a penny worth?" One cent. "How many pennies do we have?" Five. "How many cents are the five pennies worth?" 5 cents. "How much is the nickel worth?" 5 cents.
3. "Five pennies are worth 5 cents and one nickel is worth 5 cents." Repeat this statement together several times.

4. Now instruct your child to count five pennies into your hand. Hold the pennies in that hand and ask her to put the nickel in your other hand.

5. Open your hands and show her the coins. How many cents are the five pennies worth? How many cents is the nickel worth? "Five pennies will buy the same amount as one nickel."

Snacks for 5 cents

1. Show your child a box of snack crackers. Pretend that each cracker costs 1 cent. Let her buy crackers one at a time and place them on her napkin until the pennies are used up. How many crackers did you buy with five pennies? Lay the five pennies beside the five crackers.

2. Now let your child buy five crackers at once with the nickel and place them on another napkin. How many crackers did you buy with the nickel? Lay the nickel beside those five crackers. "Five pennies will buy the same amount as one nickel."

3. Now pour a small cup of juice and pretend that the juice costs 5 cents. Let your child choose to buy juice with either five pennies or one nickel.

4. Enjoy the crackers and juice for a snack. Let your child buy more juice with the coin(s) she didn't choose before. "Five pennies will buy the same amount as one nickel."

MoneySkills

✔The cents value of a coin tells us what we can exchange it for.

✔When something costs 5 cents, we can pay with one nickel or five pennies.

---

15. Games with Coin Equivalents

These short games give your child practice exchanging the right coins to buy something for 5 cents or 10 cents.

Coin equivalents for 5 cents

1. Ask your child to hold out his hand. Count five pennies into his hand.

2. Lay several coins on the table. "Which coin equals those five pennies in your hand?" Have him hold the nickel in the other hand.

3. Now pretend you are a storekeeper. Show your child an item he can buy for 5 cents, perhaps a balloon or piece of candy. "Which hand do you want to use to pay for the balloon?"

4. Allow your child to pay with the nickel or the five pennies. Explain that each is the same as 5 cents.
5. Use real money to make a chart showing a nickel at the top and five pennies beneath. Put the nickel chart up in your child's room where he can review it often.

Coin equivalents for 10 cents

1. Use the steps above to introduce other coin equivalents: "Ten pennies will buy the same amount as one dime." "Two nickels will buy the same amount as one dime."
2. Play bank teller. Allow the child to exchange a dime for two nickels or 10 pennies. Then switch roles and let the child be the teller. Review coin equivalents introduced before.
3. Make a chart showing that a dime equals two nickels or 10 pennies. Put the dime chart up in your child's room next to the nickel chart. Encourage your child to review the charts daily.

Introducing other equivalents

As you introduce additional coin equivalents, continue playing the store-keeper and bank teller games and making charts. Be patient as the coin combinations get more complicated. It takes time for children to grasp these concepts!

MoneySkills

✔When something costs 10 cents, we can pay with one dime, 10 pennies, or two nickels.

✔It makes no difference which coins we use to pay, as long as we pay the correct amount.

---

16. Teddy Bear Playground

This activity makes it fun to practice buying things that cost 25 cents!

How to set up a teddy bear playground

Look for things around the house that a teddy bear could ride in: toy trucks, a doll carriage, a wagon, or a shoebox pulled by a rope. Let your child have fun inventing other rides. Then arrange the rides in a large circle or in rows, and help your child make signs for the playground and tickets for the rides.

How to operate a teddy bear playground

1. Before the teddy bear can ride, he must buy a ticket for 25 cents from your child (the "ticket keeper").
2. Make three wallets for the teddy bear by folding sheets of construction paper in half and taping the ends.
3. Show your child how to put a quarter in one wallet, 25 pennies in another, and five nickels in the third.
4. Explain that each wallet contains 25 cents—exactly enough to buy one ticket. Which wallet will the bear choose to pay for his first ride?
5. Continue the game, letting the teddy bear choose a different wallet to pay each time he needs a ticket.

For more fun

Play this game on the swingset in your back yard or at the park. Pretend to be at a carnival where teddy bears and children must pay to ride on the swings. Vary the ticket prices according to your child's present skill with coin equivalents.

Make a quarter chart

Make a chart showing that a quarter equals 25 pennies or five nickels. (Some children will also be ready to see that a quarter equals two dimes and one nickel.) Hang the new chart beside the others in your child's room and review it often.

MoneySkills

✔Twenty-five cents is the same as one quarter, five nickels, or 25 pennies.

✔To count money, we count the cents value of the coins, not just the number of coins.

---

17. Money Line

The money line is a creative way to illustrate coin equations so children actually see, hear, and "feel" the concepts they are learning.

Here's how to get ready

1. For this activity you will need solid-colored fabric scraps (five different colors), a fabric marker, clothespins, and clothesline or heavy twine.

2. Let your child help you cut the fabric into squares:

Color 1: Ten 3-inch squares
Color 2: Five 4-inch squares
Color 3: Ten 5-inch squares
Color 4: Four 6-inch squares
Color 5: One 7-inch square and one
2-inch square

3. Use the fabric marker to draw as large a circle as possible on each square of fabric except for the 7-inch square and the 2-inch square.

4. Label the 3-inch circles to represent pennies, the 4-inch circles as nickels, the 5-inch circles as dimes, and the 6-inch circles as quarters.

5. On the 7-inch square, draw a rectangle and label it to represent a dollar bill. Draw an equal sign (=) on the 2-inch square.

6. String a clothesline between two chairs or across the corner of a room.

How to play with clothesline money equations

1. Start with pennies. Ask your child to hang five "pennies" on the line.

2. Then show your child the equal sign and explain that it means "the same as." What are five pennies the same as? Five pennies are the same as one nickel.

3. Now the child hangs up the equal sign and one of the "nickels." Count the pennies again. Say together, "Five pennies are the same as one nickel."

4. As your child is ready, use the same steps to show coin equivalent statements for a dime and then a quarter.

For more challenge with the money line

1. Write the money equations on slips of paper and put them in a basket. Let your child draw an equation and see how fast he can hang the equation on the money line.

2. Have your child turn his back while you put up a "mystery" equation. Then let him turn around and see how fast he can read the equation and lay out real coins to match.

3. Add fabric squares to the game to teach more advanced money equations as your child grows older.

MoneySkills

✔We can understand and illustrate basic money equations.

✔We can count to see if a money equation is right.

---

18. 100 Pennies

Explain to your child that it takes 100 pennies to make one dollar bill. Take your child to the bank. Show her how you exchange one dollar bill for 100 pennies (two rolls).

When you get home, dump all the pennies on the table and look at them. "That's a lot of pennies! Can you count 100 pennies?"

How to practice counting

1. Put the pennies is a plastic margarine bowl with a lid.
2. Give your child a second plastic bowl. Let her practice counting as many pennies as she can into the bowl until she makes a mistake.
3. With practice, she will count more and more pennies correctly each day. Tell her there is going to be a prize when she can count all 100 pennies.
4. When she can count all 100 pennies correctly for five days in a row, take her to the store and let her buy something with them: balloons, animal crackers, peanuts, or sugarless bubblegum. Help her select something that costs under $1 and let her pay the clerk. Leftover pennies can go in your child's piggy bank.

MoneySkills
✔When something costs $1, we can pay with one dollar bill or 100 pennies.
✔We can count 100 pennies correctly.

Activities That Teach Money *Smarts*

Most of what we teach preschoolers about money are basic "money mechanics"—recognizing coins, calling them by their correct names, and counting coins. This body of knowledge is the basis for learning to be *money smart*.

Being money smart is being responsible. The coin bank we used with Activity 3 taught a simple principle of money smarts: *We keep money in a safe place.* As your child enters kindergarten, you will see a sudden leap in her ability to be responsible. This is the time to introduce money smart activities.

Introducing your child to money responsibility

1. Show your child what a paycheck looks like.
2. Talk about why you go to work every day.
3. Take your child to the bank with you to deposit your paycheck.
4. Then take your child with you to buy groceries. Explain that your paycheck buys things the family needs.
5. Show your child the utility bills and how you write the checks and mail in the payments.
6. Talk about ways people earn money—different kinds of jobs people do. The teller at the bank earns money for her job. The checker at the grocery store is working at a job. Watch for people in different jobs and occupations.
7. Try to make a time to take your child to visit your office or place of work.

Banks are friendly places

When you take your child to the bank, she probably won't understand all the transactions going on there, but she will know it is an important place. Talk about how you put your money in the bank or credit union to keep it safe.

Introduce your child to a teller or a bank officer who handles your accounts. They almost always have time to show a future customer around, and they like to give out candy and balloons!

---

19. The Banking Game

Bob Leibel, a financial consultant in San Diego, Calif., invented this banking game to teach his 5-year-old grandson how working, paying for things we need, and banking all fit together. When Bob's grandson arrives for a visit now, the first thing he wants to do is play *their* game.

Getting ready

1. Play money: Use the play coins and dollar bills you made in earlier activities. Let your child make some additional bills in large denominations: fives, tens, twenties, fifties, and hundreds (or buy some inexpensive play money.)

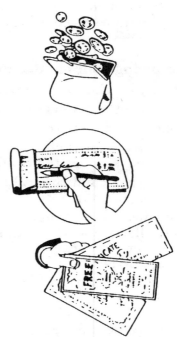

2. Things to represent banking activities: an old checkbook cover, leftover deposit slips, a small scratch pad for the "teller" to make receipts for deposits.

3. Pretend checkbooks: Staple several strips of paper together at the top. Draw lines and label the places to fill out the check. Or make one master sheet of checks. Photocopy, cut apart, and staple into "books." For children who aren't ready to fill out checks, make play checks for set amounts: $5, $10, $20. Then the child only has to "sign" the check.

4. Advertising coupons and certificates: Save coupons you get in the mail, in the paper, or find displayed at stores. Examples: free oil change, half-price chicken dinner, free eye examination, buy one hamburger—get one free.

How the game works

1. Start the game by pretending to pay your child some large amount of money for "working." Count out a bunch of play money and hand it to your child.

2. Let your child pretend to deposit all or part of the money in the bank, which you have established in a certain place across the room. He fills out a deposit slip, gives the "teller" the money, and waits for his receipt.

3. Then your child can pretend to pay bills, buy groceries, hire people to fix things, visit the doctor, take his children to the pony rides, or anything his imagination conjures up. You play along and act out various roles as he directs the action.

4. Everything your child buys costs money. He will have to decide whether to pay with play money or "write a check."

5. If he runs out of money, he will have to go back to the bank and withdraw more. He will eventually have to "work" to earn more money.

How to use the advertising coupons

The advertising coupons represent the various jobs your child can choose to do for more money. For example, if your child picks the free oil change coupon, he will pretend to drive your car to the garage, put it up on the racks, and change the oil. When he returns with the car, you inspect the job, and pay him for his work. If your child picks the buy-one-get-one-free hamburger, he will pretend to work in a restaurant and cook you a hamburger. This game can go on and on with endless variations. Bob says his grandson plays the game all afternoon while Bob keeps one eye on the football game!

TODAY'S DATE
_____

TINY TOT BANK
1901 SMITH ST.
ANYTOWN, U.S.A.

PAY TO THE
ORDER OF

TEN DOLLARS AND 00 CENT **$ 10.00**

AMOUNT

YOUR NAME

TODAY'S DATE
_____

TINY TOT BANK
1901 SMITH ST.
ANYTOWN, U.S.A.

PAY TO THE
ORDER OF

TWENTY DOLLARS AND 00 CENT **$ 20.00**

AMOUNT

YOUR NAME

MoneySkills

✔We "deposit" our money in the bank so it will
  be safe until we need it.
✔We pay for things with the money we earn,
  either using cash or writing checks.
✔When we write a check, we are taking our
  money out of the bank.

20. First Allowance

Games are excellent tools for preparing children to handle money, but they are not a substitute for the experience of managing and spending *real* money. According to child development experts, an allowance is the *number one* tool for teaching children to manage money. You should start giving your child an allowance when she is 5 years old or first entering school.

How much?

The purpose of an allowance is to give your child practice making spending decisions. If the allowance is not large enough to make any decisions, your child won't learn anything. So think of the allowance as an investment in your child's education. The amount should be enough to spend, but not enough to require financial decisions beyond your child's abilities. The average allowance for 5-year-olds is between 50 cents and $1.

Make it a special occasion!

- Getting your first allowance is a momentous occasion, so make it special!
- Invite your child to go out with you to breakfast. Talk about how she's growing up, that it's time for her to get some practice handling money, and that you are going to give her an allowance.
- Explain that this money is your child's share of the family income and it is hers to spend as she wishes, as long as she doesn't use the money for things that are dangerous or harmful.

The agreement

Agree upon a certain day, time, and place when the allowance will be given. Then live up to that agreement. It is easy for parents to get busy, not have the right change, or just outright forget allowance time. (How would you feel if your boss forgot your paycheck half the time?) Be a good example of dependability by paying the allowance on time—*every* time.

MoneySkills

✔An allowance is my share of the family income.

✔It is my responsibility to manage my allowance.

✔It is my parents' responsibility to pay the allowance at the same time and place each week.

---

21. Family Chores

When it's time for your child's first allowance, the question of chores and their relationship to the allowance must be considered. *Should kids do chores to earn their allowance?*

What child development experts say

Some parents feel that children should do something to earn their allowance. So they tie certain household chores to the allowance. This system works for some families, but child development authorities say children should do chores because they are part of the family, not because they will be paid.

John Rosemond, a noted family psychologist who has been researching and writing about parenting for more than 15 years, explains why. He says chores are to teach kids responsibility, and an allowance is to teach them money management. Parents should not confuse the issues by making receiving an allowance contingent on doing certain chores.

Everyone does chores!

Children should be taught from an early age that everyone in the family does chores. A child of 3 can pick up toys, help clear the table, feed pets, and put laundry in the basket. A 5-year-old can help set the table, fold towels and washcloths, empty trash cans, and learn to make his bed. If your child doesn't have a chore list, it's time to start one now.

1. Make a chart listing three or four simple chores your child can do each day.
2. If your child doesn't read, draw a simple picture or symbol beside each chore so he can easily identify the job.
3. Then make squares to place stars or checks when each chore is completed.
4. Reward your child with lots of praise. He is a very important member of the family!

MoneySkills

✔We do chores because we are members of the family, not to be paid.
✔The family depends on me to do my part.

---

22. Rent a Kid

Allowances are given to children so they can learn to budget—not so they can buy everything they want. However, there are times when kids legitimately need more money. How can we see that our children have extra money when they truly need it without undermining the allowance system?

Harold Moe, author of **Teach Your Child the Value of Money** (Harsand Press) recommends a plan he calls Extra Income Opportunities. It's simple. Help your child *earn* the extra money by hiring her to do extra "beyond-the-call-of-duty" jobs (not regular chores) that need to be done around the house.

Here's how it works for preschoolers

1. Make a short list of extra jobs your child can do around the house for a set amount of money—usually only a few nickels or dimes at this age. If your child doesn't read, draw pictures or symbols to help her recognize the jobs.

2. Post the list on the refrigerator or the family bulletin board. When your child needs extra money, she can select a job from the list. The choice must be entirely the child's. These are not required chores— they are opportunities!

3. When the job is completed, your child is to ask you to look over her work. Always show appreciation and say something to praise her for her effort!

4. If you feel the job needs to be improved, offer suggestions or show her how. We cannot expect small children to do the job as well as an adult, but we do want children to try their best and be proud.

Getting paid

Keep a jar of change hidden so you can pay your child as the job is completed. *Important!* A young child does not understand being paid "later" and will not connect being paid for her work unless paid immediately.

MoneySkills

✔When I need extra money, I do extra work.

✔We get paid for doing good work, so it is important to do my best.

✔The work I do is important because it helps my family.

---

23. Three Banks

If you don't teach your child anything else about money, teach her to *save!* Use three banks to help your preschooler understand "money we save," "money we spend," and "money we give."

How to set up a system of three banks

1. When your child starts receiving an allowance, give her three banks. Help her paste pictures, draw symbols, and decorate the banks. Label the banks Saving, Spending, and Sharing.

2. Explain each bank. The Saving bank is money that stays in the bank and keeps accumulating until you need it for something special. The Spending bank is everyday spending money. The Sharing bank is money we set aside to help others (charity).

3. Use coins when you pay allowance or extra jobs. If she gets 15 cents for a job, help her put one nickel in the Savings bank, one in the Spending bank, and one in the Sharing bank. You can show her how to save, spend, and share part of everything she earns.

What happens?

* After a few weeks, ask your child to lift each bank. The Saving bank will get heavier each week, but the Spending bank will probably stay very light. Kids like to spend every time they get near a store!

* Explain that when you *spend* money it is gone. You have traded it for something else. When you save money, it grows. Then you can buy something better or worth more.

* Money in the Sharing bank should be saved to help someone less fortunate. Demonstrate giving as a part of your family life. Let your child learn the joy of giving from the heart.

MoneySkills

✔ We like to save part of our money for special goals.

✔ When we spend money, it is gone.

✔ Our family shares part of our money with others.

---

24. Quick Trips

Teaching through everyday events can be as simple as a trip to the bank, a stop at your neighbor's garage sale, or going to rent a movie. Each of these excursions offers a chance to learn about money. The secret is to take the time to explore the potential learning opportunities in these everyday events and to involve your child in informal discussions about what he saw and heard.

Everyday learning opportunities
- A ride in a taxi or on a bus
- A peek in the kitchen at your favorite restaurant
- A sample of the newest flavor at the ice-cream shop
- An hour watching workers at a construction site
- A look in the stockroom of your favorite toy store
- A visit to the fire station
- A drive by the lake to see the boats and people fishing
- A quick trip to the bakery

Informal discussions

Go to explore, to enjoy the sights, and to learn something interesting. Talk about what you see, the jobs being done, how people earn money, use tools, how the workers dress and travel to work every day.

Spend some time that evening recounting the events of your visit. Small children may not remember or understand every word you say, but they will remember attitudes and values about work, money, and people.

Make a poster
1. Collect magazines with pictures of people working, studying, playing sports, involved in daily activities.
2. Ask your child to find and cut out pictures of people doing things he wants to do when he grows up.
3. Then use the pictures to make a poster titled "Things I Will Do When I Grow Up" or "What I Will Be When I Grow Up." Display the posters where the whole family can admire them.

MoneySkills
✔People do many kinds of jobs to earn money to take care of their families.
✔I can choose what kind of work I want to do when I grow up.

---

25. Fixing Things

Encouraging young entrepreneurs begins long before they are actually ready to start mowing the neighbor's yard. It starts with teaching very young children to enjoy work and to have confidence in their ability to do a good job.

Give your child tools

1. Give your child a tool box with a real hammer, screwdriver, and pliers for a birthday or holiday. As your child gets older give her a new tool each holiday.

2. Prepare a board with partially started nails and screws, leaving a lot of space between. Then show your child how to hold a nail with the pliers (not small fingers) and hammer it in. Explain that the claw on the hammer is to remove crooked nails. Show her how to use the screwdriver for the screws and the pliers to straighten screws that start going wrong.

3. Give your child a special outfit to wear when she works. Or help her make a work shirt by decorating an old T-shirt with designs that remind her of work.

4. When repairs around the house are to be done, invite your child to bring her tool box along and help. Young children can start by handing you the right tool and watching. Granted, it will take longer to let a child help pound a nail or repair the sink, but you will be rewarded by the smile of pride on your child's face when she says, "Look what we fixed!"

Built-in opportunities

Maintaining a home provides hundreds of opportunities to show your child that "fixing things" and solving problems is rewarding. Other work: plumbing repairs, changing the oil on your car, fixing a flat on a bike, changing the belt on a vacuum cleaner, tightening screws, pounding in loose boards on the fence. All these things are great adventures for a young child!

MoneySkills

✔Everyone can learn to use tools and do small repair jobs.

✔Doing our own work to fix things around the house saves us money.

For More Information

Math connection

Preschoolers love to count and work with numbers. Basic math skills are essential in working with money. The U.S. Dept. of Education has a free brochure to help make math fun at home. Request "Help Your Child Learn Math" by sending a self-addressed, stamped, #10 business envelope to: National Council of Teachers of Mathematics, 1906 Association Drive, Reston, VA 22091

Creativity

How do we nourish creativity in children? For a free brochure (limit: 1) full of ideas, request "High, Wide and Deep" from: Hogg Foundation for Mental Health, The University of Texas, Austin, TX 78713-7998

Building self-esteem

Children need to see themselves as valued, respected persons. For a free brochure (limit: 1) on this subject, request "Caring: Building Children's Self-Esteem" from: Hogg Foundation for Mental Health, The University of Texas, Austin, TX 78713-7998

Home activities to reinforce learning

A free booklet is available to parents who want ideas on how to prepare children to learn. Request "Parent Child Education—At Home—At School" from: Early Childhood Education Advisor, 333 Market St., Harrisburg, PA 17126-0333

Math motivation

Receive a handbook of teaching aids you can use at home to make math fun. Request "Polishing Children's Math Skills" from: Early Childhood Education Advisor, Pennsylvania Dept. of Education, 333 Market St., Harrisburg, PA 17126-0333

Make today special

Need a boost to get you out of those humdrum days? Request "Today Cards" from: Early Childhood Education Advisor, Pennsylvania Dept. of Education, 333 Market St., Harrisburg, PA 17126-0333

Children at play

Play is essential for a child to learn. For guidelines on encouraging play that is valuable and appropriate, request the brochure "Play is FUNdamental" (#576). Send 50 cents to: Natl. Assn. for the Education of Young Children, 1834 Connecticut Ave. NW, Washington, DC 20009-5786

Further Resources for Teaching Children Ages 3 to 5

How Much is A Million? by David M. Schwartz, Lothrop, Lee & Shepard Books, 1985. A beautifully illustrated picture book for young children. Text and pictures explain the concepts of million, billion, and trillion. Author's notes in the back explain how the calculations were made.

If You Made A Million by David M. Schwartz, Lothrop, Lee & Shepard Books, 1989. Illustrations by Steven Kellogg make this a book young children will love, even if they do not understand all the words. Coins are pictured and their value explained. The book relays how various amounts of money from 1 cent to $1 million could be spent. It also introduces checking accounts, savings accounts, loans, interest, and taxes. Notes from the author guide parents on how to use the book.

Teach Your Child the Value of Money by Harold & Sandy Moe, Harsand Financial Press, 1987. An excellent book outlining steps to teaching children successful money management, mechanics, and savings habits. It includes how to recognize teaching opportunities in everyday family life, how to motivate with a three-part allowance, and how to teach your child the magic of compounding savings.

The Kidfun Activity Book by Sharla Feldscher, Harper & Row, 1990. More than 250 easy activities requiring little or no equipment for ages 2 1/2 through 8. Hundreds of suggestions for making everyday events pleasurable times. A very warm-hearted and delightful book about having fun with your kids.

Slow and Steady, Get Me Ready: A Parent's Handbook for Children from Birth to Age 5 by June R. Oberlander, Bio-Alpha Inc., 1988. A handbook of 260 sequential activities to do at home from birth to age 5 to prepare children to enter school. The book describes a variety of ways to use household items for materials and stimulate learning through play. For parents, day care workers, baby sitters, anyone caring for young children.

Mister Rogers' Playbook: Insights and Activities for Parents and Children by Fred Rogers and Barry Head, Berkley Books, NY, 1986. An insightful and imaginative book that describes how play is vital to a child's growth. Contains over 335 games and projects for very young children and families to do together. Emphasizes helping children express themselves as they explore the world.

Mister Rogers' Plan & Playbook: Daily Activities from Mister Rogers' Neighborhood for Child Care Providers, 2nd ed., Family Communications, Inc., 1985. Outlines every activity used on the "Mister Rogers" TV program for a whole year. Helps plan daily talking and sharing times with children ages 3 to 6. Emphasis is on exploring the world and a child's feelings about the world.

Chapter 3

MoneySkills for Ages 6 to 8

There is one wonderful word to describe a 6-year-old: EAGER! A 6-year-old wants to learn everything, fears almost nothing, loves to go with you anywhere, is enthusiastic about life, and runs full speed ahead from the time he wakes in the morning until he falls exhausted into bed at night. He's a jumping, bumping, wiggling, giggling, bundle of excitement and eagerness to learn!

Introducing *MoneySkills*

A 6-year-old is standing at the threshold of life, just getting a glimpse of how big the world really is. Everything is a great adventure. He still believes in magic. And he's sure he can run faster, climb higher, and yell louder than any other kid around.

All this eagerness to "conquer the world" makes age 6 the perfect time to explore new challenges in learning about money. Now that your child has entered school, he needs money *skills*. One of the greatest challenges for a first- or second-grader will be learning to make change. Your child will also need to develop a more realistic concept about what money can buy.

By age 8, your child will be adding, subtracting, multiplying, and dividing numbers in school. He will be able to handle financial transactions with greater independence. And he will discover he can *earn* money. Eight-year-olds love buying, selling, trading, and making choices with money.

What to teach children ages 6 to 8 about money

Age 6:
- To identify bills and coins of larger denominations
- To count larger amounts of mixed coins
- To understand coin equivalents
- To make simple change
- To divide allowance between spending, saving, sharing banks

Age 7:
- To be accurate at making change
- To read price tags

- To look for things on sale
- To match appropriate amounts of money with things to buy
- To make sure he receives correct change for a purchase

Age 8:
- To estimate the total of several purchases
- To identify times he "blows" money on things that don't last
- To recognize TV commercials aren't real life
- To save toward a short-term goal (no longer than 1 month)
- To limit borrowing to important occasions
- To realize he can earn money by doing extra jobs
- To deposit money in a savings account

Make MoneySkills fun!

Now that your child is in grade school, the emphasis shifts from learning money *facts* to learning money *skills*. To understand the task your 6-to-8-year-old is about to tackle, you might think of how you would feel if you suddenly forgot how to count change, compare prices, estimate totals, or make a bank deposit. Would you be able to carry on your daily activities? Not for long!

Learning about money is a big job for a child. Parents can make it fun with games, activities, contests, and special projects like the ones described in this book. Many of the activities in this chapter involve games that give kids practice counting money and making change.

Guidelines for games

1. Rules for kids' games should be kept flexible. Allow kids to make up their own rules if they wish, as long as all players agree.
2. If you have young children playing with older children, devise handicaps so the younger kids have a fair chance. (Example: Give a younger player extra turns.)
3. Even though the object of many games is to win, help your child understand there can be only one winner. Games are played for fun. If you had fun, it was a good game!

The importance of praise

Children age 6 to 8 need lots of encouragement, praise and rewards to give them incentive to keep going. When your child has difficulty with a task, praise him for what he did accomplish. If you show frustration or make your child feel stupid, you will discourage him from learning and damage his self-esteem. Our goal is to keep kids working for the positive reward of praise instead of working because they are afraid of our displeasure.

Money and food should be used as rewards only sparingly. We do not want children to get the idea they ought to be paid for doing what is right or behaving well. We also do not want children to see food as a reward when good things happen or as a comfort when bad things happen.

There are many acceptable ways to reward children and make them feel special. One of the best is to acknowledge what your child has done well by saying, "I like the way you...put your plate by the sink/closed the door quietly/helped me carry the groceries." These simple statements reinforce and encourage desirable behaviors (even in adults!). A hug, a pat on the back, or a word of genuine praise are always appropriate rewards. Here are some creative ways to reward your child for his special efforts:

- Keep a bag of non-edible treats such as pencils, bookmarks, party favors, stickers, balloons, and giveaway items from local businesses. Let your child close his eyes and grab a treat.
- Reward a child by letting him choose a book to read, stay up 15 minutes longer, take a bubble bath, or be the leader in the next game.
- Propose a toast at family mealtime in honor of your child's good work or extraordinary effort.
- Encourage your child to share good news with a close friend his age. Make a special call to grandma or a favorite aunt.
- Capture the moment with an instant camera. Then write a caption about the event below the picture and display it on the family bulletin board.
- Have a candlelight dinner in honor of a family member who deserves recognition for a job well done.
- Give a your child a back rub or scalp massage. Talk about how much you appreciate his special efforts.
- Pick a flower from your garden and place it in a vase on the table. Place a card beside it announcing your child's special accomplishment that day.
- Give your child a special privilege such as licking the beaters when you finish making a cake, sitting at the head of the table at dinner, or choosing what kind of pizza to order.
- Serve ice cream, sherbet or pudding desserts in your best crystal to celebrate your child's good work.
- Display his special papers, drawings, art projects, or certificates of achievement on the refrigerator or bulletin board. When it's time to take them down, let your child know he's special by saving these things in a large box or scrap book.
- Buy an inexpensive picture frame and hang your child's awards on a wall in his bedroom. Make a special shelf for trophies and a box or bulletin board for ribbons.
- Don't forget the old favorites—clap hands or "high five" for the person who does a good job.
- Ask your child about words he likes to hear. Practice saying things that make people feel good: "You're right." "That's a good idea." "You sure look nice today." "Thank you for helping." "That's okay, you did your best." "I love you."
- Make gift certificate surprises. Think up 10 or 20 special privileges your child enjoys: a walk to the park, renting a movie, a trip to get an

ice-cream cone, staying up late on Saturday night, having a friend spend the night. Write these on separate pieces of paper, roll them tightly, and put them in a jar. Let your child close his eyes and pick one for a special surprise.

Perhaps this list has made you think of other special things you can do to encourage and reward your child. Why not jot them down in the margins of this page right now? Then you can refer to them often as you use the games and activities in this chapter.

Activities That Teach Money *Facts*

26. Magic Counting

Teaching your child to count nickels means she needs to know how to count by fives. To count dimes, your child needs to be good at counting by tens. Here's an outdoor game that makes it fun to practice counting by fives and tens.

A magic bridge

1. Use chalk to draw a pathway of 10 circles, about 12 inches in diameter, somewhat irregularly on the driveway or sidewalk.
2. Tell your child that the circles are a magic bridge of coins across an enchanted pond in the middle of a dark forest. You must cross the pond without falling into the water, or you'll be turned into a frog (or some other disgusting creature) forever.
3. To cross the pond, the child must hop from circle to circle counting the coins loudly by fives (or tens). If she falls off a coin or makes a mistake in counting, she has to go back and start over again from the beginning.

4. This game can be played by one child or by several children competing to see who makes it across the pond first. Add more circles as your child's counting skills increase.

More practice counting fives and tens

1. Put 10 dimes in a small plastic bowl. Let your child practice counting the dimes by tens up to $1. When she is able to count the dimes correctly five days in a row, reward her by giving her the dimes to spend.

2. Repeat the same activity with 20 nickels, teaching your child to count by fives to $1. Again, you can reward your child by allowing her to spend the nickels when she can count them correctly.

MoneySkills

✔Because a nickel is worth 5 cents, we can count nickels by counting by fives.

✔Because a dime is worth 10 cents, we can count dimes by counting by tens.

---

27. Test Your Memory

Because coins are common objects we handle every day, we rarely look at them closely. But children are very detail-minded. This memory game may show that your child remembers more about coins than you do!

How to get started

1. Show your child how to use a compass to draw circles the size of a penny, nickel, dime, and quarter on several sheets of paper. Write the names of the coins under the blank circles.

2. Now place a penny, nickel, dime, and quarter face up on the table. Give your child a few moments to look at the coins.

3. Remove the coins and ask him to draw as much as he can remember about what each coin looks like. Then you try it.

4. Look at your drawings together. This is not easy! Praise your child for the details he remembers. Encourage your child to practice until he can draw both the fronts and backs of each coin.

Have fun showing off what you know!

Help your child make extra sheets with circles for each coin. Then let your child ask adult friends or relatives to draw what is on the front and back of a coin. Your child will be very proud he can do something most adults can't do!

What makes money "official?"

- Show your child some foreign coins or some play money coins. Can we buy things at the store with these coins? No, we can't. Only coins made by our government can be used to buy things. We know coins are official when we see the right markings on the front and back.
- Tell your child to pretend he has been asked to design a new coin for the United States. How much would the coin be worth? What famous person's face would go on the front? What words would be printed on the coin? How would it look? Then ask your child to draw a picture of the coin.

MoneySkills

✔The markings on our coins let us know they are official.

✔Only official coins and bills made by the U.S. government can be used to buy things in our country.

---

28. Large Coins

First-graders are very good at recognizing pennies, nickels, dimes, quarters, and $1 bills. Your child will enjoy learning about larger coins.

How do you divide a dollar?

1. Hold a dollar bill in your hand. Ask your child, "What can we do if we want to give someone *half* of a dollar?" We can't tear dollar bills into pieces and give people parts of them, so we use coins to give people part of a dollar.
2. Show your child a half-dollar. "This coin is called a half-dollar because it is worth *half* of a dollar." We can use a half-dollar coin to give someone half of a dollar.
3. Talk about the special markings on a half-dollar: the great seal of the U.S. on the back of the coin, John F. Kennedy's picture on the front.
4. Explain that we don't see half-dollars very often because the government doesn't make very many. Half-dollars are large and heavy, and most people don't use them often.

What is a *silver* dollar?

- Explain to your child that we also have a coin that is worth one *whole* dollar. We call it a silver dollar. You can remember it because dollar bills are green and the dollar coin is silver. Silver dollars were once made of silver.
- Show your child a silver dollar. Talk about the history of the coin and how there aren't many silver dollars now because the government doesn't make them any more.

Becoming a collector

Can you buy things at the store with half-dollars and silver dollars? Sure! But most people don't. Because these coins are becoming very rare, many people save or collect them.

Give your child a half-dollar and a silver dollar to save until she has children of her own. Talk about how many years old the coins are and how their value increases each year. Help your child find a special place to keep her coins safe, or perhaps keep them for her until she is older.

MoneySkills

✔A half-dollar is worth half of a dollar bill.

✔A silver dollar is worth one whole dollar.

✔We keep rare coins in a safe place because they get more valuable each year.

---

29. Big Bills

Let your child see you use cash as much as possible. If you always use checks or credit cards, young children may get the idea that spending is free.

Kids love to see and touch big money!

Show your child our most common large bills: the $5 bill, $10 bill, and $20 bill. Do you see the presidents' names under their pictures? Which of these presidents are also pictured on coins?

What are big bills worth?

1. Lay a $5 bill on the table. "A $5 bill is the same as five $1 bills." Count five $1 bills on the table. Do the same with a $10 bill.

2. Take your child to the bank. Give the teller a $20 bill and ask for $1 bills. "We trade the $20 bill for 20 $1 bills because they are the same." Count the 20 $1 bills together.

3. Ask the teller to show your child a $50 bill and a $100 bill. Or cash a check for a large bill, spend time showing it to your child, and re-deposit it.

Make charts

Cut strips of green or brown construction paper about the size of dollar bills. Let your child draw and label the strips to represent ones, fives, tens and twenties. Then help your child make a huge poster showing dollar equivalents:

- One $5 bill is the same as five $1 bills
- One $10 bill is the same as 10 $1 bills or five $1 bills and one $5 bill.
- One $20 bill is the same as 20 $1 bills or two $10 bills or four $5 bills.

MoneySkills
✔The number in the corner of the bill tells how many dollars it is worth.
✔People like large bills because they take less room and are easier to count.

---

30. Bank Teller

Here's something to do on a rainy, boring weekend afternoon! Let your child empty his entire piggy bank on the table, floor, or bed. Show him how bank tellers count money.

How does a bank teller count all that money?

1. First make a chart with four columns. At the top of the columns tape a penny, a nickel, a dime, and a quarter.

2. Then have your child divide all the coins into piles according to their denomination.

3. Show him how to count the number of coins in each pile. Help him enter the number in the correct column on the chart.

4. If there are too many coins for your child to count at once, show him how to make a mark in the correct column as he picks up each coin. Then total the marks in each column.

5. Which pile of money is the biggest? Which column has the most marks? Multiply to find the total of each column. How much money do you have in pennies? Nickels? Dimes? And quarters?

6. Add the totals from all the columns together. How much money was in the piggy bank?

For more practice

- Keep a change jar in the kitchen. Every day put a little more loose change in the jar. Let your child be the teller who counts the money once a week and reports to the family.

- Having a garage sale? Let your child help count the money at the end of the day. Then show your child how to count out enough coins for a roll, stack the coins in the roll, and seal the rolls. If he has trouble getting rolls started, try pushing the first few coins in with a pencil.

MoneySkills

✔When counting a large amount of money, first separate the coins into piles of pennies, nickels, dimes, and quarters.

✔Then count each group of coins separately and write down the totals.

✔Add the totals from each group to find out how much money you have altogether.

---

31. Advanced Coin Equivalents

Children need lots of practice working with coin equivalents and learning to count change. You can use everyday items around the house to give your child extra practice.

Make a money tray

1. Put 10 nickels, 10 dimes, four quarters, and 25 pennies in sections of an egg carton, ice cube tray, or muffin pan.
2. Show your child a dime. Ask her to see how many ways she can count 10 cents using coins from her tray. Next show your child a quarter. Now how many ways can she find to count 25 cents?
3. Tell your child you are selling bananas (or her favorite fruit) for 25 cents each. She is to buy three bananas from you. Each costs 25 cents, but you want her to pay you three different ways. Let her count out the money to buy each banana, one at a time.
4. Gradually increase the challenge (and add more coins to the tray) until your child can count all the ways coins could be combined to make one dollar.
5. Reward your child for a super effort by giving her the right amount of change to buy something from a vending machine the next time you're out shopping.

What is your favorite way to get a dollar?

On allowance day, sit down at the kitchen table together. Place a $1 bill on the table. Then place four quarters beside the dollar. Next make a line of 10 dimes beside the quarters. Now arrange 20 nickels in a row beside the dimes. Last, make a row of 100 pennies stacked in groups of 10.

As you point to each row, let your child tell you how much the coins are worth. Since each row equals $1, does it make any difference which one you use to buy something? Ask your child which way she would you rather receive her allowance each week.

MoneySkills

✔ Coins can be combined many ways to add up to $1.

✔ It makes no difference which coins we use to buy something as long as we pay the cor rect amount.

Activities That Increase Money *Skills*

Every time your child sees a commercial on TV, it is obvious what money is for—*to spend!* On toys, cereal, and fun! It's up to parents to teach kids to think before they spend. One mother decided it was time to do something when her children kept begging for gourmet frozen dinners selling for nearly $5 each. She took them to the supermarket and showed them how to price each item in the dinner separately. They were amazed that for the price of three dinners, they could buy enough ingredients to feed the whole family the same meal, plus a whole chocolate cake, and still have money left over.

Shopping requires *skill*. Your child needs to know how to read price tags, count change, examine a product for quality, estimate totals, and tell if she has enough money. The activities in this section are designed to teach your child those skills and more. But don't forget to take advantage of opportunities to teach your child each time you go to the store together.

Suggestions for shopping with a 6- to 8-year-old

1. Save clean labels from products your child likes and paste them on sheets of construction paper. These become your child's personal shopping list. She can find the products by matching the pictures on the labels.

2. Lay ground rules before you enter the store. These also communicate important money values. "I don't have any extra money today, so we are only going to buy what is on the list."

3. Let children get practice reading numbers on price tags. Ask your child to read the prices aloud as you put things in the cart.

4. Take this opportunity to teach proper nutrition to your child. Let your child choose one item from each of the four basic food groups.

5. Ask an older child to find an item from your list and bring back to you. When she is good at that, give her two, then three. See how many things she can find without needing a reminder.

6. Standing in the checkout line is boring. Make a game of guessing how many bags it will take to sack your groceries. If the line is very long, guess how many bags it takes for the person in front of you. Was this more or less than last week?

Equipping your child to shop starts with teaching how to count money and make change. The activities in this section will make it fun to practice these skills.

---

32. Tennis Ball Contest

This game has been known to fascinate children as well as adults for long periods of time. While the kids are having fun, they'll be getting practice counting money!

How the game works

1. You'll need three tennis balls and a wastebasket. Use a marker to label the tennis balls Nickel, Dime, and Quarter. Set the wastebasket in the corner of the room.
2. Stand behind a line about 10 to 15 feet away and try to throw the balls into the wastebasket. Balls can be thrown directly into the basket or bounced against the wall.
3. Each time you make a basket, you score the amount written on that ball. The first player to reach $1 wins the game.
4. For older children, increase the challenge of counting score by adding three more balls labeled as before.

A quiet version of the game

You'll need five paper plates labeled Nickel, Two Nickels, Dime, Two Dimes, and Quarter. Place a large trash can or box on the floor. From a line 6 to 10 feet away, toss the paper plates into the container. Players total the points written on the plates that hit the target.

Counting score

- Help younger children count up their score by counting aloud with them. Teach them to start with the largest coin and go to the smallest.
- Challenge the older children by charging a penalty if they count their score wrong.

MoneySkills

✔When we count money for change, we count aloud so the other person can follow along.

✔We count change starting with the largest coins, going to the smallest.

---

33. Miniature Bowling

You can pack this game in a suitcase and take it on vacation!

How to make your game

1. Gather 10 golf tees and a button or bottle cap.

2. If all the golf tees are the same color, show your child how to use a marker to make even stripes on three, zig zag stripes on three, and wavy stripes on four.

3. Designate the even striped tees as worth a dime each, the zig zag striped tees as worth a nickel each, and the even striped tees worth a penny each.

Rules for playing the game

1. Set the golf tees up on a table like bowling pins with the even stripes in front, the zig zag stripes next, and the wavy stripes in the back.

2. Use the button or bottle cap for the bowling ball. From a line about 8 inches away, players take turns thumping or snapping the button with one finger to try to knock down all the pins. As in bowling, each player gets two "rolls."

3. The game lasts 10 "frames" or rounds. Each player must count his or her own score correctly after each frame. Help younger children count their score aloud starting with the largest coin. The player with the highest score wins.

Helping young children count score

If your child is just beginning to learn about counting money, he may need extra help keeping score. Lay out real coins to match the "pins" he knocked down. Then point to the coins together as you count the score. Use a calculator, if necessary, to check addition on the total scores.

34. Ring Toss Game

Ring toss games can be played almost anywhere and anytime. Use these variations to help your child have fun learning to count money.

How to make a miniature ring toss game

1. Make a game board from a square of thick corrugated cardboard or a sheet of styrofoam. Use a marker to draw two-inch circles in a pattern of your choice on the board.

2. Write Penny, Nickel, Dime (or 1 cent, 5 cents, etc.) in the circles. Insert one toothpick in the center of each circle.

3. Give each player five plastic rings from milk jug tops. Each player takes a turn tossing rings at the toothpicks to score points.

4. After each turn, the player must count his or her score aloud starting with the largest denomination and ending with the smallest.
5. As your child's skill increases, add more challenge to the game by charging a forfeit for counting incorrectly.

Fun ways to make more ring toss games

1. For a larger ring toss game, a stool or chair turned upside down on a table is an easy way to make a target. Players take turns attempting to throw rings over the legs.
2. Rings can often be salvaged from old games or garage sale "junk." Make rings from an old garden hose. Cut 10-14 inch lengths of hose and coil to make a circle and secure with masking tape or duct tape. You can also make rings out of rope, old belts, and heavy cardboard reinforced with tape.
3. Save liter soft drink bottles. Fill with water or sand and set them in a pattern on the floor or outside on the driveway. Label the jugs randomly: Penny, Nickel, Dime, Quarter, Half Dollar, $1, $5. The score is figured by totaling the amount of money each player "wins."

35. Beans!

What's the easiest way to give 35 cents in change? Seven nickels? Three dimes and a nickel? Or a quarter and a dime? Here's a game that gives your child plenty of practice counting change in the smallest number of coins!

How to get ready

1. Nail a tin can to a small board or piece of plywood and place it in the middle of your driveway or patio.
2. Use chalk to draw a circle with a 6-foot radius around the can. Divide the circle into fourths and number the sections. Mark a throwing line within each section.
3. Provide each player with a handful of beans, corn, or pebbles and a sheet of paper to keep score. Tell your child that every bean she gets in the can scores 5 cents.

How to play

The player stands on the throwing line in Section 1 and tosses three beans at the can. If the player gets one bean in, she gets to move to the next section and throw three more beans. She continues in this manner until she gets no beans in three throws. She removes her beans from the can and totals her score (5 cents for every bean in the can.) When the player's turn comes again, she starts from the position where she stopped before.

Scoring

Using the following score sheet, show your child how to mark the score in the correct columns using the fewest number of coins. The first player to earn $2 wins the game if her sheet is correct. If the score sheet has an error, she forfeits 5 cents for each error and the game continues.

SCORE SHEET

Score	Nickels	Dimes	Quarters	TOTALS

36. Calendar Points

Here's a wonderful way to recycle last year's calendar! Use it to make a game that helps your child learn to count money.

How the game works

1. Place a calendar with large numbers on a table. Pretend that the numbers in the squares are amounts of money your child can win.
2. Give your child three milk jug lids or bottle caps. Show him how to stand behind a line 4 to 8 feet away and toss the lids one at a time to land in the squares on the calendar.
3. Players score the number in the square where the lid lands. If a lid touches two squares, count the highest number.
4. Show your child how to mark his score using the least number of coins. To write the score of 30, put one mark under "Quarter" and one mark under "Nickel." To write the score of seven, put one mark under "Nickel" and two marks under "Pennies."

For an added challenge

It's harder to play the game in reverse! Start the game by giving each player a score of $3. After each turn, players subtract their points and tell how much money is left. The first player to "spend" all her money wins.

MoneySkills
✔When we count change, we try to use the fewest number of coins possible.
✔We count money starting with the largest coins, going to the smallest.

---

37. Backwards Bowling

Children with more advanced skills can use this bowling game to practice giving change.

Setting up the game

Collect five to 10 empty toilet paper rolls, juice cans, or oatmeal boxes. Write 5 cents, 10 cents, or 25 cents at random on the inside or bottom of each. Set these up like bowling pins at least three inches apart. Mark a line 8 to 12 feet away. Give the player a small ball.

How to bowl backwards

1. The player stands on the line with his back to the bowling pins. When you say "go," he rolls the ball between his legs and tries to knock down the pins.
2. In this game, players get one roll. Then the player must count his score aloud starting with the largest coins. The first person who gets a total of $5 wins.
3. Play the game again, keeping score the "backwards" way. Start the game giving each player a score of $5. As each player takes a turn, he subtracts his score and tells how much change he has left. The first person to "lose" all his money wins the game.

For extra help keeping score

1. Show children how to use a calculator to check their scores.
2. Keep score with play money. Here's a quick way kids can make their own: Cut sheets of paper into 3-inch wide strips for dollar bills. Cut several strips of paper into small squares and label them 5 cents, 10 cents, and 25 cents.
3. Use "backward" score keeping to practice the correct way to count change. Give each player $5 in play money. After each turn, the player pays the "banker" the amount of his score. Kids take turns being banker and counting change aloud. Later, make a rule that the banker must pay a penalty if he counts change wrong!

---

38. Super Dice

Kids like dice games, but ordinary dice are small and hard for children to read. Your child will be delighted with the "super-size" dice used to play these games.

Make three super dice

1. Dice can be made from almost anything cube-shaped. Suggestions: Salvage used blocks from an old toy box, buy blank wooden blocks at a craft store, or cut three large squares of foam from an old cushion.
2. Using a set of ordinary dice for a pattern, help your child mark with a pencil or piece of chalk the right places for dots on his dice.

3. When you are sure all the dots are marked correctly, use a permanent ink marker to color the dots. Make the dots on each dice a different color so you can tell them apart.

Now you're ready to play!

Game 1: Use one die. Let each dot equal one nickel, dime, or quarter. Take turns rolling and see who can get to $5 first.

Game 2: Use two dice. Let each dot on one equal a nickel, and each dot on the other equal a dime. Take turns rolling and see who can get to $5 first. Each player must count and add his own score correctly or lose a turn.

Game 3: Use three dice. Let each dot on the first equal a nickel, each dot on the second equal a dime, and each dot on the third equal a quarter. The player who gets $10 first wins. Each player must count and add his own score correctly or lose a turn.

Game 4: Use three dice to play Game 3 as above. This time keep score "backwards." Players start with $5. Each time a player rolls, he subtracts his score and tells how much change is left. The first player to "spend" all his money wins. Keep a calculator nearby to check answers.

MoneySkills
✔We count money starting with the largest coins, going to the smallest.
✔Counting money aloud helps us be more accurate.

---

39. Can I Buy It?

Young children have a hard time knowing if they have enough money to buy something. Here's a game to help your child practice matching small amounts of money with things she can buy.

Look for things that cost $1

1. Get two identical sale papers from a local discount store where your family likes to shop.
2. Give your child one sale paper and ask her to cut out pictures of things we can buy for a dollar or less.
3. Then let her paste all the pictures on construction paper and cut them apart.

4. Use the other sale paper to look up the prices of each item. Let your child write the prices on the backs of the pictures.

Now practice buying!

1. Put change in an empty ice tray or egg carton: five nickels, five dimes, four quarters, and 10 pennies.
2. Tell your child to look through the pictures and select something to "buy." Make it more fun by pretending to buy something for grandma or a friend's birthday.
3. You be the storekeeper. Tell the child how much she owes and see if she can count out the correct amount of change from the money tray to buy the item.

For more challenge

Show your child a certain amount of money from the tray. Ask her to count the money. Then have her look through all the pictures and show you the things she could buy with that much money. "What if I give you 10 cents more? What can you buy now?" "What if I take 25 cents away? What can you buy now?" Continue the game another day, adding new pictures and taking turns being the storekeeper and the shopper.

MoneySkills

✔We can buy things only if we have enough money.

✔We count our money and match it to the prices on things we want to buy.

---

40. Playing Store

Playing store is a favorite game for children of all ages. As your child enters grade school, the game becomes more elaborate. Your child will now use the play store to practice counting money, making change, and shopping on a budget.

Setting up a play store for grade-school children

1. Collect large cardboard boxes and set them up along one side of the child's bedroom or playroom. Wrap inexpensive shelf paper or white butcher paper around the boxes.
2. Help your child choose a name for the store and make a sign to go on the wall or door. Decorate displays and counters with sale signs and pictures from magazines.
3. Stock the store with empty boxes and packaging from food, drugstore, and household products. Help your child make price tags and tape them to the products. Keep prices realistic, but easy to count.
4. Supply the store with play money, a cash drawer, and perhaps an adding machine to make tape receipts.
5. Give your child brown paper grocery sacks to label with his store name and logo—just like real stores. Use large sheets of art paper to make sale flyers. Let the "cashier" wear something special like a name badge or an apron, vest, or bow tie.

Playing and learning

1. Make a game of reading price tags and comparing amounts. Ask your child to group items in the store by prices: 50 cents and under, $1 and under, $1 and more.
2. Let your child select things from the store to "buy." When he pays you, show him how you count the change. Then count the change aloud together. As his skills increase, switch roles.
3. Teach your child that we always count our change a second time. Just for fun, occasionally give him the wrong amount of change and see if he catches your mistake.

MoneySkills

✔We look at the prices on things we want to buy and count our money to match the price.

✔When we receive change for a purchase, we count it again to see if it is correct.

---

41. Sack Math

A group of Girl Scouts set up a play store at their school math and science fair. Visitors to their mini supermarket received $25 in play money. Whoever could come closest to spending $25 without going over won a prize.

Their booth was one of the favorites at the fair. Your child will enjoy playing this game, too!

How the game works

1. On six 3 x 5 cards write various amounts ($2, $3, $3.50) your child might spend at the play store you created for Activity 40.
2. Put the cards in a small paper sack and allow your child to draw a card. His goal is to buy a sack of groceries that comes as close to the amount on the card as possible without going over.
3. As your child shops, talk about how we "round" prices and estimate how much we are spending.
4. When he is finished choosing what he will buy, take each item out of the sack one at a time and estimate the total together. Then use a calculator to total the bill. How close was your estimate?
5. Children can compete to see who "stacks a sack" without going over.

For enrichment

1. From time to time, surprise kids with real items for the store: penny candy, bags of popcorn, miniature boxes of raisins, etc.
2. Let kids have your expired cents-off coupons for things in the store. Show them how coupons make their money go farther.
3. Play the game in reverse: Fill a sack with items from the play store and see who comes closest to the correct estimate of the total.
4. Invent other stores (toy store, restaurant) to play sack math.

MoneySkills
✔Rounding prices makes them easier to add in our head.
✔We estimate our total purchases before we go to the checkout counter to be sure we have enough money.

---

42. Toys on TV

Turn TV commercials into tools for teaching! Make a game of questioning the techniques, words, and props that make toys in ads look appealing.

Go to the store!

Take note of any toy commercials that attract your child's attention. Then go to the store, find that toy, and examine it together.

- Does it really do what they say on TV?
- Is it as much fun as it looks on TV?
- Is it appropriate for your child's age?
- Is it safe?
- Will it last?

Very often your child will see for herself it doesn't look much like what she saw on TV. Talk about how TV ads are designed to make things look fun and to make us want to buy. But TV isn't real, and sometimes we can be very disappointed.

Limit TV time

Help your child limit the number of hours she spends watching TV (and commercials) each week.

1. Read the TV schedule together and talk about what you will watch that week. Discuss which shows are better choices and why.
2. Set time limits for yourself and your child for TV watching.
3. Make a chart for each person, listing the shows you plan to watch, the date, time, and channel.
4. Follow up on your plan by making a second chart showing what you actually watched that week. How well did you do?
5. Talk about how much time you spend on various activities each day: sleeping, eating, doing chores, doing homework, playing, etc. Keep charts to see how much time you actually spend on each activity.

MoneySkills

✔TV commercials use special words, music, settings, and props to make us want to buy.

✔We should examine products closely to see if they really do what the ads claim.

---

43. Fast-Food Restaurant

Kids love to visit fast-food restaurants for hamburgers and fries. A pretend restaurant in the corner of your den or child's bedroom will peak your child's imagination and give him practice with money mechanics.

Creating your hamburger restaurant

1. Try to make your restaurant as authentic as possible. Collect reusable items like styrofoam containers, straws, paper cups and bags from your favorite fast-food restaurants.

2. Encourage your child to use his imagination to create "foods" for the restaurant. Fabric scraps can be sewn and stuffed to represent hamburgers, hot dogs, and other favorite fast-food items. Other materials that can be used are felt scraps, sheets of styrofoam, cardboard, household sponges, pipe cleaners, and pictures from magazines.

3. Staple scrap paper together to make order pads. Use posterboard to make a sign for your restaurant. Fill your cash drawer with play money, and you're ready for business.

Running your restaurant

Let family members take turns visiting the restaurant, giving their orders, and paying for their food. Your child will have to add up the total cost of the order and give correct change.

A "manager" (parent or older child) can oversee the orders and assist the child when he needs help. Let your child invite his friends over, too.

MoneySkills
✔We count money starting with the largest coins, going to the smallest.
✔Counting money aloud helps us be more accurate.

---

44. Reading Sale Papers

Kids have a great influence over the way we spend our grocery dollars, so we need to teach them to be smart shoppers! Ask your child to help you read the sale paper this week.

What's for dinner?

1. Show your child the sale paper from your favorite grocery store. Ask him to circle 3 things he would like for dinner this week.
2. While he is busy with the sale paper, take a quick inventory of the kitchen and start your grocery list. Talk about the items your child circled. Let him write the ones you decide to buy on the grocery list.
3. When you go to the store, ask your child to help you find the items he chose. Let him mark them off the list.
4. On future shopping trips, ask your child to read the sale paper again. You might ask him to circle three things he likes for snacks or circle three things to pack in his lunch.

What does "one-fourth off" mean?

Children in early grades have no idea what sale slogans like "one-fourth off" mean. Here's a hands-on way to explain it.

1. Show your child a cookie and a single slice of American cheese. Tell your child to pretend that he wants to buy the cookie. The slice of cheese is our money.
2. In order to get the cookie you have to give the storekeeper your whole slice of cheese. (Pretend to trade the cheese for the cookie.)
3. But today the cookie is on sale! It's one-fourth off. (Show your child how to break the cheese into fourths.) That means you get to keep one-fourth of the cheese for yourself and give the storekeeper the other three-fourths. (Trade three-fourths of the cheese for the cookie.)
4. Now eat the cheese *and* the cookie for a snack!

> *MoneySkills*
> ✔Smart shoppers plan what they are going to buy *before* they go to the store.
> ✔Buying things on sale helps us save money.

45. Treasure Hunt: Comparison Shopping

The next time you have a birthday or holiday gift to buy, invite your child on a "treasure hunt" to find the best price. This activity is a good way to introduce the concept of comparison shopping to a younger child or encourage an older child who spends money too freely to slow down and plan her purchases.

Shopping to learn

1. First decide on a specific item you are going to buy (a compact disc player for Dad's birthday).
2. Tell your child you are taking her on a "treasure hunt" to find the best price for the CD player. Offer your child a reward for doing the research to find the best price.
3. Visit three stores that have the CD player in stock. Give your child a small notebook and put her in charge of writing down the price at each store.
4. Now study your research. Which was the lowest price? Which was the highest price? Where will you buy the gift? How much will you save?

It pays to hunt bargains!

1. Give your child tangible evidence that it really pays to shop for bargains. As a reward for her work, pay your child the difference (or a percentage of the difference) between the highest and lowest prices you found.
2. Talk about the results of your treasure hunt: (1) You got the best price for the CD player; (2) Your child learned to be smart shopper; and (3) She earned some money for her work!

Note: This activity is recommended to be used sparingly and should be initiated only by parents for specific learning occasions.

MoneySkills

✔ Smart shoppers check at least 3 stores to find the lowest price before they make a purchase.

✔ Saving money when I shop means I have money left over to use for other things.

---

46. Do-It-Yourself Halloween

Holidays give families many opportunities to practice being smart consumers. Encourage your kids to make do-it-yourself costumes for Halloween. Being creative is a lot more fun—and it costs less! Use the money you save to take the family to a carnival or go out to eat.

Home-made costume ideas

- Clown: Dad's old dress shirt, a loud tie, bright red or yellow sweat pants, and oversize tennis shoes.
- Pirate: Old pants turned into knee breeches, a man's shirt turned backward with the collar turned in, a scarf tied at the neck, and an old tablecloth, skirt, or curtain for a cape.
- Rabbit: Add a hat with floppy ears and a fluffy tail to a child's one-piece sleeper.
- Fairy princess: Old formals or dresses.
- Turn a large box into a costume. You can be a robot, a jack-in-the-box, a TV, or a typewriter.

Halloween makeup

Save small margarine bowls or baby food jars. In each jar, mix one tablespoon of old-fashioned cold cream, two teaspoons of cornstarch, and one teaspoon of water. Add a few drops of food coloring and mix. Leave one jar white for painting clown faces. Remove makeup by wiping with tissues.

Start a dress-up collection

Other costumes easily constructed from things you find at home are cheerleader, hobo, gypsy, scarecrow, ballerina, scientist, and rock star.

Collect old hats, costume jewelry, ribbons, purses, makeup, and props throughout the year. Watch garage sales, resale shops, and thrift stores for inexpensive items to add to your dress-up box.

MoneySkills

✔When we save money by making things at home, we have more money to spend on other things.

✔Don't throw away anything without thinking how it might be used another way.

---

47. The Great Pumpkin

Kids love to carve jack-o'-lanterns at Halloween. Use this pumpkin project to teach your child how to get more value out of a dollar.

Selecting the right pumpkin

1. About three weeks before Halloween, give your child the job of watching the grocery sale papers for the best buy on pumpkins. Make a chart to compare the price of pumpkins at several stores. Let your child enter the prices in columns for Week 1, 2, and 3.

2. When you spot the best buy, make a special event of going to select the "great" pumpkin. Choose one that will make a good jack-o'-lantern and also be suitable for Thanksgiving pies.

3. If the pumpkin is priced by the pound, show your child how to weigh produce and estimate the cost of your purchase. When you check out, watch to see if you were right.

Making a jack-o'-lantern

1. Since pumpkins spoil easily, don't carve the jack-o'-lantern until the day before Halloween. If your child needs practice or can't wait for Halloween, let her practice on apples or potatoes.

2. Consider decorating instead of carving the pumpkin. Use markers, acrylic paints, clown makeup, or cake decorating icing. A carrot can become a long nose. A bell pepper cut in half makes good ears. Use yarn for hair or give your pumpkin a hat to wear.

More for your money

- Roasted pumpkin seeds make a healthy snack to offset all the Halloween candy you eat. Spread the seeds on a cookie sheet and roast at 350 degrees for about 15 minutes or until they are golden brown. Seeds can also be dried naturally, painted, and strung into necklaces.

- The day after Halloween, clean the pumpkin well and cut it in large chunks. Steam it in a small amount of water on the stove or in the microwave. When the pumpkin is tender, let it cool and scrape the pulp off the rind. Freeze to make pumpkin pies.

MoneySkills

✔ To buy something by the pound, multiply the price per pound by the number of pounds to get the total cost.

✔ We save money by making something useful out of things we ordinarily throw away.

Activities That Teach Money *Smarts*

While you are teaching your child the necessary money skills for operating in this society, you will also want to help her get started on healthy money habits. We call these *money smarts*.

One of the most important money smarts you can give your child is a healthy attitude about credit. Your child needs practice living within her means (allowance plus extra jobs). However, special occasions will arise when your child legitimately needs more money before allowance day.

When your child asks for a loan or advance on next week's allowance, you have the opportunity (and obligation!) to teach your child about the wise use of credit. Look over the following suggested credit guidelines and decide now what your "credit policy" will be.

Guidelines for kids and credit

1. Borrowing next week's allowance should not be a habit.
2. The loan amount should not exceed one week's allowance.
3. Do not allow your child to become entrapped in hopeless debt. Repayment should be within one month.
4. Expect your child to pay a certain amount on the loan from each allowance until the loan is completely paid.
5. If your child falls behind on loan payments, withhold the delinquent amount from next week's allowance.
6. For older kids, charge interest and late fees.
7. If you allow your child to borrow an amount more than one week's allowance, post a list of extra jobs he can do to earn the money.
8. Teach your kids that borrowing is a privilege and must be earned.

Kids may gripe about your terms, but don't give in. Credit is a very serious problem in our society. Responsible parents must take aggressive action to teach this generation to earn or save money *before* spending it!

48. Allowance Day

Here's a plan that will give your child more opportunity to make wise financial decisions.

Provide a built-in planning period

1. Give out allowances on a day in the middle of the week.
2. Show your child how to make lists of ways he plans to spend his money.
3. Encourage him to check ads, compare prices, and think about the choices he can make when the weekend comes.
4. Plan when and where you will shop.
5. Expect him to change his mind several times during the week. Explain that this is part of learning to make good choices.

Learning from decision making

- Before you decide how much to give your child for an allowance, ask: What do I want my child to learn by receiving and managing a weekly allowance? Do I want my child to have spending money only? Money to save? Money to give to charity? To buy gifts? Then estimate the amount it will take to give your child those learning opportunities.

- Once you give your child his allowance, he must make choices and experience the consequences of his decisions. This doesn't mean you can't give hints or suggestions, but don't let the allowance become an emotional power struggle between you and your child.

- You probably won't always agree with the way your child spends his allowance, but he will learn from his mistakes. If he insists, let him buy that toy you know he will break before he gets home. After all, the best time to make mistakes is now, while the child is still young.

MoneySkills

✔I don't need to spend money right away.

✔I make better choices about money when I take time to plan.

✔I like to shop where I get the lowest price.

---

49. Daily Duties

The experts say we should teach our children that everyone does chores because they are members of the family, not to be paid. So how can we get kids to do their chores if we can't threaten to cut off their allowance?

Make kids feel important!

1. Talk about the importance of each person's contribution.
2. Make sure the duties you assign your child are not just "busy work." Your child needs to know she is a vital part of the family—that what she does is important.
3. If your child fails to do her job, don't do it for her. With encouragement and communication, she will eventually require fewer reminders. Be generous with patience and praise.

Have a plan!

1. Children age 6 to 8 can be expected to do simple chores that take no longer than 5 to 10 minutes each. Make a list of daily and/or weekly chores that are appropriate for your child's age and ability.
2. Next, make a 3 x 5 card for each chore, describing the chore in detail, what cleaning product or tools to use, and when the job should be completed. Some parents like to color code the cards (e.g., yellow for daily, pink for twice a week, blue for weekly).
3. Let your child help make a "pocket" poster for her chore cards. At the top of a piece of posterboard, write "Daily Duties." At the bottom, glue two envelopes labeled "To Do" and "Done." In the middle, draw squares for each day of the week.
4. Every morning, put the chore cards for the day in the envelope marked "To Do." As your child completes each chore, she should move it to the envelope marked "Done." When the chores are completed, put a star or sticker in the square for that day.
5. Surprise your child occasionally with cards with special treats like "Take your favorite book to Mom for 15 minutes of reading time."

MoneySkills

✔ Just as each person shares in the family fortune, each shares in responsibilities.

✔ The family depends on me to do my part.

✔ We help because we are members of the family, not because we expect to be paid.

---

50. Birthday Privileges

Here's a way to make your child feel special! Start a tradition of taking your birthday child out to breakfast or lunch so you can have time to talk alone. Birthdays are ideal times for introducing new privileges and responsibilities.

Talking together

1. Talk about the good things your child has accomplished that year, why you are proud of him, and what an important part of the family he is.

2. Encourage your child to talk about things he would like to accomplish in the coming year, perhaps even writing a list of goals for the year.

3. Discuss new privileges and responsibilities you want to give your child since he is getting older, such as an increase in allowance, a later bedtime, starting music lessons, or allowing him to go to camp for the first time.

4. Talk about the responsibilities that come with the new privileges. (Examples: designating a percentage of his allowance for charity, checking in when he's away from home, or practicing his music lessons a certain amount each week.)

Make a record of the event!

1. To celebrate the event (and make sure there are no misunderstandings), write a list of the new privileges and responsibilities your child is receiving. Read over the list and sign it together.

2. Keep each year's birthday meeting list in a special notebook or folder so you both can look back and see the yearly, step-by-step growth toward independence.

MoneySkills

✔As I learn to be responsible, I can be trusted to manage a larger allowance.

✔My allowance is a share of the family income.

✔I should also share in the family responsibilities.

In Honor of Your Birthday

Name: _____

Age: _____

Date: _____

We're proud of you because:

Your new privileges this year are:

Your special responsibilities will be:

It's going to be a great year!

Signed: _____ (Parents)

_____ (Child)

51. Cash Gifts

Sometimes parents and grandparents like to give money for gifts at birthdays and holidays. Here are some ways to make these gifts more fun:

Fun money

1. Change the money into dollar bills. Tie each to a balloon with ribbons and dangling party favors to make a balloon bouquet. Or put the dollar bills inside the balloons before you blow them up. The birthday kid will have to pop the balloons to get the money!

2. Make a treasure hunt with clues leading your child all over the house, into the closet, under the bed, behind the couch, upstairs and downstairs. Clues can be elaborate rhymes wrapped in fancy boxes or simple statements on slips of paper: "Look in a place where you keep shoes." Disguise the cash by wrapping it in a large box weighted with canned foods or a brick.

After the party

1. Gift money should be your child's to spend as she pleases. Parents should not arbitrarily make decisions about the money, such as putting it in her college fund.

2. Take your child on a special excursion to spend her birthday money. If she decides to save part of it, stop by the bank and make your deposit before you go shopping!

3. Teach your child to write thank-you notes when she receives gifts. For young children, buy notes with verses and let them sign their name. School age children can write two or three short sentences in their own words.

Another cash gift

Start a family tradition of giving new babies in your family a framed set of coins minted the year of their birth. Then as the children are old enough, tell them the story of the coins. Even very young children love to talk about "their" money, repeat the names of the coins, and see their birthdate printed on the money.

MoneySkills

✔We let people know we appreciate their gifts by writing thank-you notes.

✔Money I get for gifts is my responsibility to spend wisely.

---

52. Throwaway Money

In Activity 23, we set up a system for your child to manage his allowance with three banks labeled Spending, Saving, and Sharing. Author and parent Bonnie Burgess Neely recommends a fourth bank to divide Spending into two parts. It's a brilliant plan that might even work for adults!

Working with three banks

As your child understands math concepts, discuss putting a certain "percentage" or "part" of each allowance dollar into his banks for Spending, Saving, and Sharing. Help young children get started by actually giving the allowance in dimes. Then use the 10/20/70 plan: one dime from each dollar in Sharing, two dimes in Saving, and seven dimes in Spending.

Talk about the Spending bank

1. Ask your child to make a list of all the things he buys with money from his Spending bank.
2. Look at the list together. Talk about things that stay around for at least one day: toys, comic books, hobby supplies, baseball cards. This is "Spending to Keep."
3. Then talk about things we buy that are gone right away: gum, candy, video game. This is "Throwaway Money."
4. Divide another sheet of paper into two columns. Label the left column "Throwaway Money" and the right column "Spending to Keep." Ask your child to look at the list of things he buys and decide which column each item goes in.

A bank for throwaway money

1. Change the label on the Spending bank to "Spending to Keep." Then make a fourth bank labeled "Throwaway Money."
2. Remind your child that he has seven dimes for spending out of each dollar. How many does he want to put in "Spending to Keep?" (Suggest five dimes.) How many does he want to put in "Throwaway Money?" (Suggest two dimes.) Having two spending banks will help him be in control of how much money he spends on things that don't last.

MoneySkills

✔Some things we buy are gone right away, and some things stay around longer.

✔We need to control how much money we spend on things that don't last.

---

53. Serious About Savings

If you want to start your child on the life-long habit of saving, show her you're serious. Help her open a savings account!

Checklist for choosing a bank

1. What is the minimum deposit required to open an account?
2. Will your child get a passbook or monthly statements?
3. How much interest is paid on accounts?
4. Are there restrictions on withdrawals?
5. Are there any service charges or fees?
6. Is a parent required to co-sign?
7. Is the bank friendly to children?
8. How convenient is the location? The hours?
9. Does the bank offer kids' saving clubs or incentives?

Opening the account

Make the day you go to the bank and open the account really special. Dress up. Take your child to the bank to sign the signature cards.

Make sure she brings something home: an I.D. card for her account, a passbook, the receipt for the deposit, a brochure about the bank. Help her find a special place at home to keep her passbook and important papers.

Make regular deposits

Once the account is open, teach your child to make deposits at least once a month. Set a date and mark it on the calendar together. Help your child find extra ways to put money aside throughout the month.

1. Make a game of picking up lost money around the house, under the bed, or in the washing machine.
2. Show your child how recycling projects can provide extra money for her savings account.
3. Suggest that your child deposit part of the money she gets for gifts.

MoneySkills

✔ We deposit our money in the bank so it will be safe until we need it.

✔ Money in a savings account grows because the bank pays us interest.

---

54. My Checking Account

"Just write a check, Dad!" Have you ever heard your child say that? Here's a fun way to show your child there has to be money in the bank to write checks.

You're rich!

Pretend with your child that you are suddenly rich. His allowance for this week is $100! The money has been deposited in his checking account. There are only three rules: 1) He may not spend the money on things that are against family health, safety, and moral standards; 2) He must spend all of the money by the end of the week; and 3) If he spends 1 cent over $100 he forfeits next week's allowance of $200. Can he do it?

The spending spree

1. Draw a sheet of blank checks with the name of an imaginary bank. Photocopy, cut apart, and staple at the top to make a pretend checkbook.
2. Give your child old catalogs and sale papers for his shopping spree. Encourage him to plan how he would spend the money before he starts writing checks.
3. Show him how to number the checks, write in the date, who the check is to, and the amount.
4. Show your child the check register in your checkbook and how you subtract each time you write a check so you know how much is left to spend. He can use the following check register to keep track of the balance in his checkbook as he shops.

The cashier's job

You are the cashier who accepts his checks for each purchase. It is your job to void purchases when the check is not properly filled out, check his "I.D.," and "call" the bank to be sure he has money to cover the checks.

To use this activity with an older child, start with $1,000 and let him pretend he is locked in a toy store all night with nothing to do but spend money!

MoneySkills

✔We deposit our money in the bank to keep it safe until we need it.

✔Writing checks takes the money out of our account and gives it to someone else.

✔We must never write a check for more than is in our account.

MY CHECK REGISTER

Check #	Date	Paid To	Amount	Balance

55. Hot Buttons

When your child finds something he wants to buy that costs more than one week's allowance—and he really, *really* wants it bad—you have found what Harold Moe, author of **Teach Your Child the Value of Money** (Harsand Press) calls a "hot button." Hot buttons are great because they give your child an incentive to learn about saving!

Make a chart

Suppose the item your child wants costs $2 and his allowance is $1 per week. Saving *all* his allowance is too much to ask a child to sacrifice. Suggest to your child that he save half of his allowance each week. To help him visualize his progress toward getting that special toy, make a chart.

1. First, find a picture to represent the item that has pushed your child's hot button. Paste the picture at the top of a piece of posterboard. Beneath the picture, write the name of the item and the price.
2. Mark off four large squares to represent the four weeks it will take to save the money. Inside each square, write the amount your child will save that week (in this example, 50 cents).
3. Staple or glue an envelope to the bottom of the poster. Each week when your child receives his allowance, he can drop two quarters in the envelope and cross off one square. And each week, he can see he is getting a little closer to reaching his goal.
4. When he puts the last quarter in the envelope, reward his efforts by taking him to the store immediately and helping him make his purchase.

The art of saving

What happens if, during the time he is saving for this special goal, he changes his mind? He doesn't want the fake rubber snake anymore. Now he wants to buy a box of army men.

Parents should keep in mind that the goal is to teach the child the benefits of saving. What he *buys* with the money is not important. What *is* important is that the child experiences the satisfaction of saving toward a goal and acquires a lifetime appreciation for the art of saving.

> *MoneySkills*
> ✔I can set goals to buy things that cost more than one week's allowance.
> ✔If I save part of each dollar I get, I can reach my goal.

56. Special Jobs

When you have special jobs or projects that you just don't have time to do, consider hiring your child. It's a good way for kids to learn new skills, get work experience, and earn extra money.

Post an ad

1. Make a sign advertising your special job, the time by which it must be completed, and the reward or pay.
2. Post your advertisement on the refrigerator door or bulletin board. If your child wants the job, she takes down the sign and reports to you for special instructions.
3. After the work is done, she should ask you to inspect the job before she is paid. Remember, the job might not get done exactly the way you would do it, but you didn't have time to do it at all!
4. Encourage others in the family (even the kids!) to advertise jobs they need done from time to time.

The best way to pay kids

Children under 12 prefer to be paid by the job, not by the hour. To most kids, an hour sounds like an eternity spent in slave labor. Kids work better if you offer $1.50 for cleaning the refrigerator, $1.75 for vacuuming out the car, and 50 cents for sweeping the driveway.

Working at home for money is one of the best ways for your child to get experience and confidence to ask neighbors for jobs when she is older.

MoneySkills

✔When I need extra money, I do extra work.

✔The work I do is important because it helps my family.

✔If I expect to get paid for work, I do my best.

---

57. Family Outings

Family outings, visits to the amusement park, and day trips are good occasions to teach your child about money.

Help your child make a spending plan

1. Several weeks before the outing, ask your child to write a list of how much money she will need for souvenirs, video games, or an extra ice-cream bar.

2. Talk about ways she can save the money from her allowance or earn the money before the outing. Then post a list of extra jobs around the house so that your child has plenty of time to earn the money she needs.

On the big day

1. Be sure your child has a safe place to carry her money when you go on the outing.

2. Set the ground rules. Make sure you know how much money she is taking and that she understands what the money is to cover. Make it clear before you go that once the money is gone, there is no more.

3. Talk to your child about questions she might ask herself before she spends money on a souvenir:

   - How long will it last?
   - Is it safe?
   - Is it a fair price?
   - Can I get the same thing for less money somewhere else?

4. Remind your child that she can look around all day and come back later when she is sure the item is what she wants.

5. You can just about count on it that after your child spends her last dime, she will see something else she wants. Don't make the mistake of giving in to her begging. The lesson she will learn about money is more valuable than any souvenir!

MoneySkills

✔I can plan ways to save or earn extra money for special occasions.

✔When I have a limited amount of money to spend, I must be careful to make good decisions.

✔When I spend all my money, there won't be any more.

---

58. The Lemonade Stand

Around the time your child is eight, he will make a wonderful discovery about himself. He's just the right age to look for ways to earn extra money! When this "awakening" occurs, his first request will likely be to have a lemonade stand.

A rite of passage

Kids today still love to have lemonade stands. It's just part of growing up! Parents may wonder if a lemonade stand is worth all the work. The answer is *yes*. The amount your child earns is not as important as what he learns.

- Money-making ventures teach children to take initiative, set goals, make plans, and be creative in solving problems.
- Your child also gets valuable experience handling money, making change, figuring expenses, and calculating profit.
- As an added bonus, he gets a taste of the business world and finds out what it's like to be an entrepreneur.

Planning

1. Lemonade stands are always more fun when several children work together. Suggest that they first make a list of things they will need: a wagon, a table or large box for the stand, signs and decorations, lemonade, cups, ice, a change box, etc.
2. Next, the children should determine how much the lemonade will cost per serving. Frozen lemonade is the most economical and the easiest to make. Remember that cups and ice are part of the expenses, too.
3. What is the lowest price you can charge for the lemonade and still make a profit? What is the highest price you can charge and still get customers? Help the children set a price that is low enough to get customers, but high enough to cover the cost of supplies and give each child some money for his work.
4. The children should spend the rest of their planning time making the booth, signs, and decorations for the table.

Tips for lemonade stands today

1. Plan your lemonade stand for the day of the week when your neighborhood is the busiest and the most customers are likely to pass your way—usually Saturday afternoon.

2. If the customers won't come to you, go to them. Put your lemonade stand on a wagon and take it to the park, tennis courts, jogging track, or the neighbor's garage sale (ask permission first!).
3. Draw attention to your stand with big signs, balloons, streamers, or a unique gimmick. (Maybe you could all dress up like clowns.)
4. Offer a really great product. Make your lemonade recipe special by adding "secret" ingredients (club soda, chopped candied fruit, etc.).

New "twists" for the old lemonade stand

1. Add a second choice: iced tea, homemade slush, orange juice, or soft drinks. Gourmet coffee or herbal tea? How about brownies, home-made cookies, arts & crafts.
2. Provide entertainment: play music, add a second booth for a puppet show, get your pets to do tricks, or give gymnastic demonstrations.
3. Add another service. Face-painting is fun! You'll need a second table, two chairs, a mirror, cold cream and tissues to remove make-up. Use leftover Halloween makeup or cheap eye shadow, eye liner, lip pencils, and blush. Practice on each other the day before your sale.

With a little imagination, a lemonade stand is guaranteed to occupy at least three kids for two solid days during the summer.

MoneySkills
✔ I can add to my allowance by finding ways to earn extra money.
✔ If the customers won't come to me, I must find a way to go to them.
✔ Entrepreneurs use their imagination to invent new ways to make products exciting.

---

59. Neighborhood Toy Sale

Overrun with toys, games and books your child has outgrown? Get together with several neighbors and help the kids put on a giant toy sale. You'll get the house cleaned up and the kids will learn valuable lessons about working together and managing money.

Getting ready

It will be the children's job to clean out their rooms and collect all the old toys, books, games and puzzles they want to sell. Parents will go in together to pay for an ad, help set up the tables, and supervise. The children will set up and run the sale as much as possible, mark prices, make change, assist customers, man the tables, and clean up afterwards.

Suggestions for success

1. Limit your sale to one day.
2. Make signs and put them up around the neighborhood.
3. Help children set prices. The usual rule is one-fourth the original cost of the item.
4. Keep each family's items on separate tables. Have a family member available to demonstrate how things work, answer questions, and negotiate with customers who want to bargain.
5. Designate one parent or an older teen to supervise the money box at all times and keep track of sales.

After the sale

Reward the kids by letting them use the money they earn from the sale to buy something they've been wanting that is not in the family budget. If this worked well, think of other ideas for sales: used book sales, plant sales, arts and crafts sales. Your child is learning to think like an entrepreneur!

MoneySkills

✔When each person does part of the work, we can get big jobs done quickly.

✔When we don't need things any more, we can sell them and use the money for something else.

---

60. Partners in Business

If investing is important to you, your child has probably already started learning the "investing vocabulary" by listening to your conversation at the dinner table. Talk to your child about how he can become a *partner* in business.

How money works for you

1. Show your child the financial pages in the newspaper. Look up companies that make his favorite foods, clothes, or games. See how much one share of stock costs.

2. Talk about what being a shareholder means. (You own part of the business!)
3. Explain how money you invest works for you while you are at school, asleep, playing, and watching TV.

Becoming a shareholder

1. Buy your child one or several shares of stock in a company with a steady record of growth. Try to choose a company that is "friendly" to stockholders, sends frequent mailings, and goes out of its way to make the small investor feel part of the company.
2. When the stock certificate comes in the mail, show it to your child and talk about why you need to keep this in a safe place. Make a photocopy for his bulletin board and let him go to the bank with you to put the real certificate in the safe deposit box.
3. Help your child find the stock symbol for his company and look up the daily stock reports in the newspaper. Make a chart for his bulletin board and show him how to write in the prices of the stock as it rises and falls.
4. If possible, take your child to actually visit "his" company or a branch office. Watch for articles in the paper about "his" company. Show him ads for his company's products in magazines and newspapers. If your child has something to say about the way the company is operating, encourage him to write a letter to the president of the corporation.
5. When the annual reports come in the mail, sit down and read them together. Your child will love the pictures even if he can't understand all the figures.

Dividend checks

One day, your child's first dividend check will arrive and you will have some decisions to make. Suggest that he save the dividend check in his savings account until he accumulates enough to buy more stock. He may want to buy more shares of the same company or "shop around" for other good companies.

Make investing real to your child and he will grow up believing that investing money is as natural as spending it!

MoneySkills

✔When we buy stock in a company, we become part owners of that company.

✔As an owner of the company, I get paid dividends on each share I hold.

✔If the price to buy a share of stock in my company goes higher than I paid, I could choose to sell my stock and make a profit.

MY STOCK RECORD

Company Name:

Symbol:
_____

Purchase Date:

 # Shares:
_____

Date	Purchase Price	Closing Price	Difference

For More Information

The money factory

Need help explaining how the U.S. Dept. of Treasury makes our coins and dollar bills? You can share this interesting color brochure with your child. Request "The Money Factory" and an accompanying pamphlet for adults, "Production of Government Securities" from: Office of External Affairs, Bureau of Engraving and Printing, Department of the Treasury, Washington, DC 20228

Facts about money

This free pamphlet will help parents brush up on the facts about money. It summarizes the basic facts about our currency and makes the information easy to find. Request "Fundamental Facts about United States Money" from: Public Information Dept., Federal Reserve Bank of Atlanta, 104 Marietta St., NW, Atlanta, GA 30303-2713

Designs on the dollar

Receive a free four-page pamphlet that tells all about our dollar bills, the symbolism behind the designs, and how to understand the serial numbers. Request "Dollar Points" by sending a postcard to: Publications, T-6, Federal Reserve Bank of Boston, P.O. Box 2076, Boston, MA 02106-2076

Discontinued currency

Get free pamphlets that tell the story of our two-dollar bill and the Susan B. Anthony coin. Request "Two Dollar Points" and "Dollar Coin Points" by sending a postcard to: Publications, T-6, Federal Reserve Bank of Boston, P.O. Box 2076, Boston, MA 02106-2076

A penny saved

Receive a free pamphlet describing the history of the penny. Good information for coin collectors! Request "Penny Points" by sending a postcard to: Publications, T-6, Federal Reserve Bank of Boston, P.O. Box 2076, Boston, MA 02106-2076

Federal reserve banks work 24 hours a day

Receive a free book that tells the story of a typical day of work at the Federal Reserve Bank of New York. Photos show workers on the job. Request "A Day at the Fed" from: Federal Reserve Bank of New York, Public Information Dept., 33 Liberty St., New York, NY 10045

The work of a federal reserve bank

The Philadelphia Federal Reserve Bank processes about 3.8 million checks every day. How do they do it? Pictures and interesting text describe the process in this free book. Request "All in a Day's Work" from: Public Information Dept., Federal Reserve Bank of Philadelphia, P.O. Box 66, Philadelphia, PA 19105-0066

The fed's gold vault

In a vault nearly one-half the length of a football field, the Federal Reserve Bank of New York holds the world's largest known accumulation of gold. Receive a free booklet that tells about the mysteries of gold and the work-a-day operations of the Fed's gold vault. Request "Key to the Gold Vault" from: Federal Reserve Bank of New York, Public Information Dept., 33 Liberty St., New York, NY 10045

Counterfeit money

Receive a free pamphlet describing what to look for in a counterfeit bill and what to do if you receive one. Request "Counterfeit" from: Federal Reserve Bank of Chicago, Public Information Center, P.O. Box 834, Chicago, IL 60690

Further Resources for Teaching Ages 6 to 8

From Gold to Money, by Ali Mitgutsch, Carolrhoda Books, 1985. An easy-reader picture book for early grades. Describes the early barter system and how people started trading pieces of gold. Discusses how coins were first made. Color illustrations.

Every Kid's Guide to Intelligent Spending, by Joy Berry, Children's Press, Chicago, 1988. For ages 8 to 12. Explains how manufacturers and merchants use advertising and packaging to sell their products, how to get your money's worth, and how to return unwanted merchandise. An excellent book for parents and children to enjoy together. Full color illustrations on every page.

A Kid's Guide to Managing Money, by Joy Wilt, Children's Press, 1979. Story of money, good ideas on earning money, and what to do with it when you get it. An easy-reader picture book for early grades. Color illustrations.

MegaSkills: How Families Can Help Children Succeed in School and Beyond, by Dr. Dorothy Rich, Houghton Mifflin Co., 1988. The purpose of book is to teach life skills or qualities that prepare children for success: confidence, motivation, effort, responsibility, initiative, perseverance, caring, common sense, problem solving and more. Activities are for ages 4 to 12.

Erasing the Guilt, by Nancy Haug and Nancy D. Wright, Career Press, 1991. Provides sensible solutions if you're a parent who wants to play an active role in your child's education no matter how busy you are. Excellent advice on how to set up time-saving routines in the home.

The Mother's Almanac II: Your Child from Six to Twelve, by Marguerite Kelly, Doubleday, 1989. A comprehensive look at children in the middle years. Activities, insights, and how parents can teach children good values and habits.

Families Learning Together, The Home and School Institute, 1201 16th Street, NW, Washington, DC 20036, 1980. A program of 48 activities for parents and kids ages 5 to 12 to do at home. "Recipes for learning" use everyday objects found in the kitchen, the supermarket, and the neighborhood to help improve math and reading skills, study skills, decision making, and confidence.

101 Amusing Ways to Develop Your Child's Thinking Skills and Creativity, by Sarina Simon, Lowell House, 1989. Activities for preschool to third grade designed to provide hours of creative fun and turn a child into a lifelong learner.

Practical Parenting Tips for School-age Years, by Vicki Lansky, Bantam Books, 1985. More than 1,000 parent-tested ideas to help guide kids ages 6 to 12 through the "golden years" of growing up. Includes valuable advice on everything from starting school to music lessons to handling allowances.

Chapter 4

MoneySkills for Ages 9 to 12

A 9-year-old has discovered the joy of doing things himself. He loves to make plans, is a fanatic about details, and delights in proving his independence. The best word to describe the self-sufficient 9-year-old is CAPABLE.

Here come the 'tweens

Just about the time your child celebrates his ninth birthday, he enters into a great struggle to be "grown-up." He is not a little child and not a teenager. He's in-between. Kids between the ages 9 and 12 have been dubbed "the 'tweens." What are they like?

- They are smart, capable, and aware.
- The mall is one of their favorite places to go.
- Most 'tweens have bank accounts.
- Most earn their money or save from their allowances.
- If they aren't spending their money, they are influencing their parents' spending habits on purchases from toys and cereals to household appliances and stereo equipment.
- They may spend more than adults on clothes, but they want to look just like all their friends.
- They are extremely loyal to the next trend.
- They can easily become victims of the media, overwhelmed by the influence of what they see on TV, in movies and magazines.
- When asked about values in a survey, a high percentage of these kids list family as tops. That means there's still hope for parents who want to influence a 'tween!

What to teach kids ages 9 to 12 about money

Age 9:
- To keep a money diary
- To make a simple spending plan for the week
- To allocate money for expenses into separate envelopes or banks
- To compare prices when shopping

- To cooperate with family efforts to save water, gas, etc.
- To look for ways to earn extra money for special goals

Age 10:
- To save a small amount each week for a large expense
- To read and understand sale ads in the paper
- To use the phone book and call stores for information
- To be comfortable asking questions when considering a purchase
- To look at the value, not just the cost, of products
- To be aware of how peer pressure affects decisions

Age 11:
- To save money for longer periods in a savings account
- To understand the principle of compound interest
- To understand fixed expenses and flexible expenses
- To adjust flexible expenses to stay within a spending plan
- To shop classified ads for bargains on used items
- To look for *facts* in TV advertising

Age 12:
- To devise and operate on a two-week spending plan
- To understand and use correct terms for banking transactions
- To understand the value of wise investing
- To recognize advertising techniques
- To read fabric-care labels and examine clothing for quality
- To operate a small business enterprise for one month

Facing peer pressure

Peer pressure to buy certain things, wear certain clothes, or associate with a certain group starts early. "But everyone else has one!" "I don't want to look like a dork!" "My friends at school wear these all the time."

Parents lecture. Kids beg. Both agree peer pressure is a problem. The important thing is to face it *together*. A certain amount of peer pressure is good. It can motivate us to try harder and work faster. One of the best ways to become an expert at an activity, sport or skill is to copy a pro or successful role model. Kids are *supposed* to be like other kids. If they're not, look at your child's social development. Are you causing your child to be an outsider by refusing to let her dress or act to fit in with her peers?

As a parent however, you resent spending a great deal of money on something that is only a trend or a fad. You know that a $100 pair of boots will be outgrown or out of style in only a few months. When your child insists on a certain brand name—which of course, costs twice as much—you are faced with a dilemma. Do I spend more money, or do I say no? If I spend more money, will I have enough left to pay the bills? If I say no, will my child become a social outcast? Which is worse?

Six ways to combat undesirable peer pressure

1. Have your child write a list of every reason she should be allowed the purchase or privilege she is requesting. Kids often realize they are being ridiculous after this exercise.
2. Make it a policy never to buy anything over a certain amount (say $50 or $100) without going home and thinking about it first.
3. Give your child a budget. "You have $200 to spend. If you choose to buy expensive brand names, you'll just have fewer clothes and have to wash them more often."
4. Get acquainted with other parents. Compare notes. Find out what's really going on.
5. Give your child a way out. Tell her to blame it on you. "My parents won't let me" is an excuse your kids can use without being embarrassed or trapped in a situation.
6. Praise your child when she thinks for herself and shows strength of character.

Everyday learning opportunities

Now that your child is older, opportunities to learn about money are abundant. Older children can and should be included in family discussions about major purchases. Now is the time to talk with your child about value, not just cost, when you go shopping.

Recreation, hobbies, and school activities are very important at this age. After-school clubs and organizations provide opportunities to practice handling money: collecting dues, soliciting contributions, fundraising, and keeping accurate records. Some of the groups offer badges or units of study on money and personal finance.

Because effective money management depends a great deal on good math skills, parents should find ways to emphasize math skills at home and show kids how math applies to everyday life. Here are some typical family situations you might present to your child as money-sense exercises:

1. Your child has 75 cents to spend. Jawbreakers are 5 cents each. How many can he buy? How much does he need for sales tax?
2. The ad in the paper says video games are 20 percent off. What is the sale price of the game your child wants? How much money will he save when he buys at the sale price?
3. The family takes a long weekend. You pay $55 for a motel the first night, $62 the second, and $48 the third. What is the average price you paid for motels on your trip?

Kids in upper-elementary grades enjoy family games that use money. A few old favorites are Monopoly, Stocks and Bonds, Masterpiece, and The Game of Life. Don't rush out and spend money buying these games new. This is another opportunity to teach your child how to use resources wisely. Make it a family project to find the games you want at a moving sale, garage sale, or resale shop.

Talk with your child about news articles and current events that affect prices. How will a hard freeze in Florida affect the price of the orange juice we have for breakfast next month? This chapter is packed with more ideas for using ordinary, objects and events to teach your child about money.

Activities That Teach Money *Facts*

61. Symbols on the Dollar Bill

When your child was in preschool, she learned that each of our coins and bills has special pictures and markings that help us identify them. Older grade-school children will enjoy learning about the symbolism of the markings on our $1 bill.

What is the Great Seal?

1. Look at the back of a $1 bill together. The two circles show the front and back of the Great Seal of the United States. Our national bird, the bald eagle, is on the face. An unfinished pyramid is on the back.
2. Explain that many countries use a special stamp or seal on their documents and government papers to let everyone know they are official. The Great Seal of the United States stands for the power and authority of our government.
3. Because the front of the Great Seal is our "coat of arms," it is used frequently. The dollar bill is the only place the government uses both the front and back of the seal.
4. Pretend together that you want to create an official seal to symbolize the unity of your family. What would you include in the design? Use pencil and paper to sketch your own great seal.

Groups of 13

The Great Seal was adopted in 1782. If you look very closely, you will find many things in the Great Seal grouped in sets of 13 to symbolize the original 13 colonies. Give your child a dollar and a magnifying glass. Set a timer for 5 minutes. See how many sets of 13 she can find. Then check your answers:

- 13 stars in the "cloud burst" above the eagle's head
- 13 stripes in the shield on the eagle's breast

- 13 berries on the olive branch in the eagle's right claw
- 13 leaves on the olive branch in the eagle's right claw
- 13 arrows in the eagle's left claw
- 13 letters in the motto on the ribbon in the eagle's beak
- 13 rows of stones in the unfinished pyramid
- 13 letters in the Latin motto above the pyramid

MoneySkills

✔The two circles on the back of our $1 bill show the Great Seal of the United States.

✔The Great Seal symbolizes the power and authority of the United States.

✔Groups of 13 in the Great Seal symbolize the original 13 colonies.

---

62. Mystery Numbers

Look at the face of a $1 bill. The large numbers in the corner of the bill tell you this bill is worth one U.S. dollar. But what do all those other numbers and symbols on the bill mean?

Solve these mysteries

1. Show your child a $1 bill. Ask your child to pretend he is a detective. His assignment is to find out everything he can about where this dollar bill was printed and released.

2. Talk about how large sheets of dollar bills are printed on huge printing presses, but each bill has its own numbers that indicate where it was printed, when it was printed, and what bank released the bill.

3. The picture on the next page will give you all the clues you need to solve the "mystery" of the numbers, symbols and words on the front of the bill. Study it together. Now ask your child these questions:

- What is the serial number of the bill?
- What year was it printed?
- What is the Federal Reserve Code letter?
- What Federal Reserve bank issued this?
- What is the Federal Reserve district number?
- Where is the Treasury Seal on this bill?

MoneySkills

Why would we need to know the serial number of a bill?

1. Stolen money is often traced by the serial numbers on the bills.
2. The numbers also help identify counterfeit bills.
3. Mutilated money that is returned to banks can be replaced if the serial number can be read.

> ### *MoneySkills*
> ✔Every dollar bill has its own serial number.
> ✔The numbers, seals, and letters on the bill give information about where and when the bill was printed.

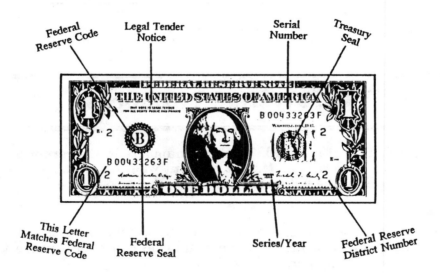

FEDERAL RESERVE BANKS

District	Code	Location
1	A	Boston
2	B	New York
3	C	Philadelphia
4	D	Cleveland
5	E	Richmond
6	F	Atlanta
7	G	Chicago
8	H	St. Louis
9	I	Minneapolis
10	J	Kansas City
11	K	Dallas
12	L	San Francisco

63. Money Trivia

Remembering facts about money is fun when you play Money Trivia. We have provided 100 trivia statements on the next few pages. You can choose 50 to start your game. Add the rest later.

How to make the game cards and board

1. Use 3 x 5 cards in three or more colors. Write the trivia statements on the cards, alternating colors. The first part of the statement goes on the front. The second part (the answer) goes on the back. Mark the backs with a star in one corner.
2. Let your child help make a gameboard on a large piece of posterboard. Draw a path of steps around the board. Use pictures from a magazine (or draw pictures) to represent a house on one side (where you START) and a bank on the opposite side. Pictures of stores, buildings, and people can be added along the path.
3. Color the steps on the path, alternating the same colors on the cards.

How to play the game

1. Shuffle the game cards and lay the deck face up in the middle of the board.
2. The player draws a card from the top of the deck and reads the statement on the front. Without looking at the back, she gives the answer. If correct, the player advances to the next step on the path the same color as her card. If incorrect, the player goes back to the previous step the same color as her card.
3. Each time a player passes the bank, her "bank account" increases by $10. When all the cards are used up, the game is over. The player with the most money in her account wins.

Other ways to play

Turn the whole room into a giant gameboard. Lay sheets of construction paper the same color as the cards in a path around the room. Players are the "markers." As an alternative to color coding, use dice or a spinner from another game to determine how far players advance.

100 Money Trivia Statements

Before money

1. Before money people got things by / trading things they had for things they needed or wanted.
2. Bartering is / trading things we have for other things we want or need.

3. Cowrie shells were used for money by / the Chinese.
4. Tea was used for money by / the Mongolians.
5. Salt was used for money by / Ethiopians and Romans.
6. Cacao beans were used for money / in Mexico.
7. Polished shells strung together was / Indian money called wampum.
8. The lightest money ever used was / feathers (on the island of Santa Cruz).
9. The heaviest money ever used was / 12 ft. stones (on the island of Yap).
10. Tobacco leaves were used as money in / Virginia and Maryland in the 1700s and 1800s.

First coins

11. Metal was first used as money 5000 years ago in / Mesopotamia.
12. Metal money was best because / it was easy to carry and lasted a long time.
13. A place where money is made is / a mint.
14. The smallest coins ever used were / Greek "obelas" that were smaller than an apple seed.
15. The first country to use gold for money was / ancient Lydia (now part of Turkey).
16. In ancient history, banks were in / religious temples.
17. The first piggy banks were made of / a clay called "pygg."
18. The first American colonists used foreign coins because / they didn't have anything else.
19. The first U.S. mint was established in / Philadelphia (in 1792).
20. Eagles, half-eagles, and quarter eagles were / early American gold coins.
21. To keep people from shaving edges off gold and silver coins / ridges were made on the edges.
22. Coins with ridges on the edges are called / milled coins.
23. The Lincoln penny was issued to celebrate / Lincoln's 100th birthday (in 1909).

Today's money

24. Today all paper money in the U.S. is issued by / the Treasury Department.
25. The special green ink on a dollar bill is made from / a secret formula.
26. The paper used to make dollar bills is / a special blend of linen and cotton.
27. Making phony money and presenting it as real is called / counterfeiting.
28. The largest bill ever printed by the U.S. was / the $100,000 bill.
29. The largest bill printed today is / the $100 bill.
30. Bank tellers sort paper bills with the portrait turned / face up.
31. Most of America's gold is kept at / an army base in Kentucky called Fort Knox.
32. Pure gold is called / 24-karat gold.
33. 14-karat gold is / 14 parts pure gold and 10 parts silver and copper.
34. Today, pennies are made of / copper-coated zinc alloy.

35. Nickels are a mixture of / copper and nickel.
36. Dimes and quarters have / a copper core covered with an alloy of copper and nickel.
37. The average life of a $1 bill is / about 18 months.
38. The government bank system that oversees all banking in the U.S. is / The Federal Reserve System.
39. Damaged and worn money is returned to / a Federal Reserve Bank.
40. Mutilated bills can be replaced if / you still have half of the bill.

Heads & tails

41. The man's picture on the face of the penny is / Abraham Lincoln.
42. The picture on the back of the penny is / the Lincoln Memorial.
43. The man's picture on the face of the nickel is / Thomas Jefferson.
44. The picture on the back of the nickel is / Monticello (Thomas Jefferson's home).
45. The man's picture on the face of the dime is / Franklin D. Roosevelt.
46. The picture on the back of the dime is / the torch and olive branch.
47. The man's picture on the face of the quarter is / George Washington.
48. The picture on the back of a quarter is / the American eagle.
49. The man's picture on the face of the half-dollar is / John F. Kennedy.
50. The picture on the back of the half-dollar is / the Great Seal of the U.S.
51. The man pictured on the $1 bill is / George Washington.
52. The man pictured on the $5 bill is / Abraham Lincoln.
53. The man pictured on the $10 bill is / Alexander Hamilton.
54. The man pictured on the $20 bill is / Andrew Jackson.
55. The man pictured on the $50 bill is / Ulysses S. Grant.
56. The man pictured on the $100 bill is / Benjamin Franklin.

World money

57. U.S. currency is based on / the dollar.
58. The currency in France is called / a franc.
59. The currency in Germany is called / a mark.
60. The currency in Japan is called / a yen.
61. The currency in India is called / a rupee.
62. The currency in England is called / a pound.
63. The currency in Mexico is called / a peso.
64. The currency in Italy is called / a lira.
65. The currency in Kenya is called / a shilling.
66. The currency in China is called / a yuan.
67. The currency in Israel is called / a shekel.
68. The most widely circulated currency in the world is / the U.S. dollar.

Symbols on the $1 bill

69. The two circles on the back of our $1 dollar bill show / the Great Seal of the U.S.
70. The Great Seal symbolizes / the power and authority of the U.S.
71. The groups of 13 in the Great Seal symbolize / the original 13 colonies.
72. On the Great Seal, the olive branch in the eagle's right claw stands for / peace.
73. On the Great Seal, the 13 arrows in the eagle's left claw stands for / war.
74. On the Great Seal, the eagle's head turned toward the olive branch symbolizes / a desire for peace.
75. The Latin motto *E Pluribus Unum* means / "Out of Many, One."
76. The unfinished pyramid on the back of a $1 bill is a symbol of / strength and future growth.
77. The sunburst and eye above the pyramid on the back of a $1 bill represents / the eternal eye of God.
78. The Roman numeral at the base of the pyramid on the back of a $1 bill shows the date / 1776, the year our country was founded.

Money words

79. Someone who is extremely careful about spending every penny is said to be / a penny pincher.
80. The lowest price you will take for something is called / your "bottom dollar."
81. A numismatist is someone who / collects coins for a hobby.
82. Someone who starts his or her own business is / an entrepreneur.
83. The tax you pay when you buy things at the store is / sales tax.
84. Someone who buys something from a business is called a / customer.
85. People who invest money in a company are called / stockholders.
86. A person who helps people buy stock is / a stockbroker.
87. Stock that costs less than a dollar per share is called / penny stock.
88. The money earned by your shares of stock is / a dividend.
89. A budget is / a plan for managing your money.
90. When you buy something now and promise to pay for it later, you are / buying on credit.
91. A plastic card that proves you have a credit account is called / a credit card.
92. When you owe money to someone or to a store, you have a / debt.
93. Interest is a fee you pay for / borrowing money.
94. When you put money in the bank you fill out a / deposit slip.
95. The money in your savings account earns / interest.
96. To take money out of a savings account you fill out a / withdrawal slip.
97. Your written order to take money out of your checking account and give it to a specific person is / a check.

98. A machine where you use a card to get cash from your bank account is / an Automated Teller Machine (ATM).

99. A written order that you purchase at a bank or post office to pay money to someone is / a money order.

100. Special checks that you take with you on a trip because they can be cashed anywhere are / traveler's checks.

(**Note:** For more interesting money facts to add to your trivia game, study the resources listed at the end of each chapter.)

MoneySkills

✔Before money was invented, people got things by trading.

✔Metal and paper money work better because they are easy to carry and easy to count.

✔We need to understand the words used to describe money transactions.

---

64. Coin Collecting as a Hobby

Coin collecting is a fascinating hobby many people start as children and continue throughout life. Coins also teach us the history of our nation.

Getting kids interested

1. Save change from your pockets each day in a coffee can or large jar. When your child needs something to do on a rainy day, bring out the can of coins.

2. Ask your child to sort the coins by years. As he works, he will notice that coins have different markings according to the years they were minted. Talk about how coins are redesigned from time to time and why.

3. Next weekend, go to the library for a book that tells how to start a coin collection, or visit a local coin shop with your child.

4. Help your child make a coin collecting "kit." He will need a magnifying glass to study the details on coins and a soft toothbrush, a soft cloth, and mild hand soap to clean coins. He will also need paper envelopes or inexpensive coin holders to store the coins. Suggestion for first collection: Lincoln-head pennies (1909 to present).

Foreign money

Visit a coin shop or a coin collectors convention. Look for displays of foreign money. Pick one or two favorite countries and learn the names of their coins. Can you spend foreign money at our grocery store? Why not?

MoneySkills
- ✔Rare coins are worth much more than their face value.
- ✔Coins collectors keep their coins clean and safely stored to preserve their value.

Activities That Increase Money *Skills*

Since children ages 9 to 12 have a great influence on family spending decisions, it is vital that parents spend time helping them develop good shopping skills. Here are some suggestions for helping your child to develop an awareness of how much things cost at the grocery store, and perhaps to cut down on the requests for over-priced fad foods advertised directly to the younger set.

Shopping with a 9 to 12 year old

1. Show your child how to read the unit pricing stickers on the shelves below products. Which is the best buy: A 16-oz. box of crackers for $1.19 or a 20-oz. box of crackers for $1.50?
2. No unit pricing stickers? Teach your child how to figure the unit prices with a calculator.
3. Let older children take turns being in charge of organizing cents-off coupons for a week or month. When you shop, it will be your child's job to help you decide which coupons to use. Pay kids 20 to 50 percent of what you save when they help.
4. Give your child two or three coupons and ask him to find the items. If your store is doubling or tripling coupons, make a game of seeing how many items you can get free or nearly free.
5. Have children who carry lunch to school plan a menu for the week and make a shopping list. Help your child compare costs and nutritional values (the four food groups).

6. Teach your child to ask these questions before he buys:
   - Is this for someone my age?
   - How much is in the package?
   - How long will it last?
   - Is there anything I don't like?
   - Is there anything that can harm me?
7. Ask kids to guess how much the final bill will be when you check out. Or give each kid a calculator and make it a game to see who comes closest to the actual total.
8. Appoint your child "store detective." As you unload the groceries, let him check each item on the receipt. Let him go with you to get errors corrected.

65. Super Shopper

The amount your family spends on groceries each week takes a big bite out of the paycheck. Help your child understand (and appreciate!) the value of being a smart shopper.

Use sale papers for research before shopping

1. Give your child the sale paper from your favorite grocery store and ask her to circle 8 to 10 foods she would like to have for lunch or dinner this week.
2. Now look at the sale paper for another store. Use a different colored marker to circle the foods she chose that are listed in both papers.
3. Show your child how to make a simple chart listing the foods that appear in both papers, and each store's price. How many prices are the same? How many times did "Store A" have the best price? How many times did "Store B" have the best price?
4. If you went to Store A and bought all of the items, how much would you pay? If you went to Store B and bought all of the items, how much would you pay? Which store saves you the most money?
5. Now for an extra challenge, figure how much you would save if you went to both stores and bought only the items that were the best price. Is it worth going to both stores?

School lunches teach smart shopping

- How does the cost of a lunch from home compare to buying lunch at school? Show your child how to estimate the average cost of a lunch from home to see how much she saves each week.

• Some parents like to give kids an incentive to make their own lunches. You provide the "fixin's." If she makes the lunches, she can pocket the money she saves by carrying a lunch. How much can she earn? How much more can she earn if she finds the items for her lunch *on sale* this week?

MoneySkills

✔We have more money for other things when we compare prices and shop at the stores that save us money.

✔We save money by doing work for ourselves (making our own lunch) rather than paying someone else to do it (buying a lunch).

---

66. Phone Book Games

A very important tool for being a smart shopper is the phone book. Older children can learn to use the phone book, look up numbers, and call stores to compare prices.

Getting acquainted with the phone book

1. Look at your phone book together. Point out that the phone book has two parts: the white pages and the yellow pages.

2. Explain that we use the white pages when we know the name of the person or business we want to call. Show your child how to find the listings for your family, friends, and favorite stores.

3. Explain that we use the yellow pages when we don't know the name of the store or business we want to call. Show your child how the businesses are listed by the *types* of services or products they sell.

4. Look up the listing for restaurants together. Can you find your favorite pizza restaurant on the list? Now look up other businesses your child likes. (Suggestions: theaters, music stores, toy stores, or sporting goods stores.)

5. Make a game of naming a product or service and letting your child guess how it would be listed in the yellow pages.

6. Show your child how to use the index to the yellow pages to see how something he wants is listed. Then show him that many entries have suggestions for other places to look.

Have a contest

- Challenge your child and a friend to see who can find things in the phone book first. You'll need two phone books of the same edition. Players sit at a table with a closed phone book in front of them and hands in their laps. You call out a listing and say "go." The first to find the listing in the phone book gets five points. Game ends at 50 points.
- Use a kitchen timer or stop watch to play this game with one child. When you say "go," set the timer for one to two minutes. When your child beats the timer, he gets 10 points. As your child's skill increases, adjust the timer accordingly.

MoneySkills

✔I can save time and money by finding stores in the phone book and calling to compare prices for something I want to buy.

✔I use the white pages when I know the name of the store and the yellow pages when I need to look up a product or service.

---

67. Back-to-School Shopping

Shopping for back-to-school clothes is an opportunity to show your child how to stick to a budget and get the most for your money. In fact, these shopping guidelines make good sense any time of the year.

Set the limits

1. Spend some time together going through your child's closet and drawers to reorganize and make notes on what she needs.
2. Tell your child to start watching and saving back-to-school sale ads from the paper. Have her make a list of the stores where you are most likely to find the best buys.
3. Discuss how much money is in the budget for clothes. Then look over the shopping list together and star the things your child needs most.

4. Now look at the ads you saved and estimate how much it will cost to buy everything you starred. How much will you have left for other things on the list?

Shopping smart

1. As you shop, discuss things to watch for when buying clothes: fit, room to grow, quality construction, care instructions, styles that last no matter what the fad, colors that compliment the hair and skin, clothes that just make you feel *good*.

2. Teach your child to look at the fabric content labels. Most manmade fibers add durability and easy care (no ironing!) qualities to our clothing. Natural fibers are best for comfort, ventilation, and avoiding skin allergy reactions. Which ones do you like best?

3. If that pair of designer jeans seems extremely important to your child, propose a compromise. You pay half if the child saves for the other half.

4. Stop for a hamburger or pizza. Spend some time talking about the coming school year and your child's special plans and dreams.

MoneySkills

✔When shopping on a budget, we first buy the things we need most.

✔Before buying an item of clothing, always examine it closely for proper fit and quality workmanship.

---

68. Make Your Best Deal

Adapted from a popular TV game show, this is a game the whole family will enjoy. It gives everyone practice in estimating costs.

Getting ready

1. Let your child cut pictures of all kinds of household products, toys, sports equipment, clothes, etc. from magazines, catalogs, or newspapers. Glue each to a 3 x 5 card and write the price on the back.

2. Make a gameboard. Draw three doors on a sheet of posterboard. Cut the doors on three sides so they can be opened and closed. Number the

doors. Behind the doors glue sheets of construction paper to make a pocket that will hold the prize cards.

How the game works

1. Start the game by shuffling and dealing the cards into three equal stacks. Without looking at the cards, put them into envelopes labeled Door #1, Door #2, and Door #3. Put the envelopes in the pockets behind the correct doors.

2. The first player chooses a door, opens it, and takes out his prize packet. Without looking at the prices on the back of the cards, he guesses how much he thinks the "deal" is worth and writes the amount down on the score sheet. Two more players choose doors and do the same.

3. Then all the players look at the prices on the backs of their cards and add them to get the total. The player whose guess was closest to the real value of his prizes is the winner.

For more fun

* Prize cards can be changed or new ones added from time to time so that interest in the game continues.
* For younger children, use fewer prizes and round the prices to make them easy to add.

MoneySkills
✔Rounding prices makes them easier to add in our head.
✔We can estimate the total of our purchases to see if we have enough money.

---

69. Watermelon-omics

Almost every kid loves watermelon. Why then do we eat watermelon only at certain times of the year? The answer to this question is a lesson in watermelon economics.

Growing seasons

1. Show your child a watermelon seed. If you wanted to plant this seed and grow your own watermelons, when do you suppose would be the best time of year? (When it's warm.)

2. It takes nearly three months to grow a watermelon. If you want to eat watermelon at the Fourth of July picnic, when does the watermelon seed have to be planted? (In early April.)
3. Because watermelons require a long, hot growing season, they can only be grown during the spring and summer in places where the climate is warm. Look at a globe or map together. What parts of the U.S. are warm enough to grow watermelons?
4. During the watermelon growing season, there are lots of melons in all the stores and the prices go down. When it gets too cold to grow melons, only a few are left and the prices go up. Fresh fruits and vegetables always cost less when they are "in season." That's why we eat most of our watermelon in the summer—especially at Fourth of July picnics.

Track prices

Ask your child to pick three of her favorite fruits or vegetables. Start a project to track the price changes from week to week and season to season on these three items. Set up a chart. Check prices when you do your weekly grocery shopping. Note the date and price on your chart. Later you can draw a graph to show the changes in price.

What other things influence prices on fruits and vegetables? Storms, drought, heavy freezes, unseasonal rains, bugs, and disease can destroy crops. With your child, check your newspaper for articles about crop failures or shortages caused by natural disasters. Read the articles together. Then watch the prices and see if they go up.

MoneySkills

✔We like to buy fresh fruits and vegetables when they are "in season" because the prices are lower and the produce tastes better.

✔Crop failures caused by natural disasters can also cause prices on fruits and vegetables to go up.

PRICE TRACKING CHART
(ITEM:) _____

Week #	Date	Price	Difference

70. Holiday Menu Planning

Menu planning, shopping, and cooking are always more fun at holidays. Don't do it all yourself. Involve the kids. It's a great time to practice their skills of planning, organization, and money management.

Making choices

1. First, write down lots of ideas. Ask your child to list his favorite holiday foods. Look through recipe books together. Talk about special dishes you've eaten other places.

2. Making choices from all these good foods is going to be hard. What do we need to consider as we plan this menu?

- Nutrition: Even at holidays it's important to plan a balanced meal that includes all four food groups.
- Budget: Holiday foods can be very expensive. Set a budget for your meal.
- Time: Choose some dishes that can be prepared ahead of time and some to cook that day.

3. List the proposed menu on the left-hand side of a sheet of paper. Start with the main dish, then add the side dishes, salad, bread, beverages, and desserts. Make three columns to the right. In the first, indicate the food group. In the second, estimate the time for preparation. The third is for estimating the cost. Review the menu, and make adjustments as necessary.

Involve kids in every step

- Have your child help you look up all the recipes and make a master grocery list. Then look through the grocery sale papers to see which stores have the best prices. When you go shopping, give your child a list of things to find. Show him how to compare brands and prices.
- Involve your child in the food preparation as much as possible. Kids are very good at helping bake cookies, make salads, stir gravy, make centerpieces, and set the table.

MoneySkills

✔Planning a holiday meal in advance allows you time to budget and make wise decisions.

✔When planning a menu, we need to consider nutrition, the family food budget, and time needed for preparation.

---

71. The Label Game

Children need to learn to read labels and make decisions about foods they eat. This activity makes it fun to learn about ingredient labels.

How to play

1. Save labels and ingredient lists from 10 favorite foods. Select from breakfast cereals, snack foods, and packaged meals.

2. Have your child number a sheet of paper from 1 to 10. Then read the ingredient lists one by one. Let your child see if she can guess the products. As she writes down her guesses, you write down the correct answers. Then compare your lists.

3. Show your child that the ingredients are always listed in order according to the proportion they are used in the product. The first ingredient listed is always the dominant ingredient in the product.

4. Now play the game again. How many did you get right this time?

More interesting clues

- Read more labels together. What vegetable do you get the most of in a can of mixed vegetables? Is chicken the main ingredient in chicken soup? What is the main ingredient in a hot dog?

- Look at the ingredients listed on various juice products. Some are 100% pure fruit juice. Some are mostly water flavored with juice. Compare the nutrition labeling. Which one gives you more food value or vitamin content?

- Look at the 10 labels you used in the game. Which ingredients do not sound like food? Talk about additives that are not really food, but ingredients to keep the food from spoiling. See if you can plan a complete meal with foods that have no additives.

MoneySkills

✔We read labels on foods to get information about the ingredients.

✔The first item listed on an ingredient label is the main ingredient.

✔We get more for our money when we buy foods that are high in nutritional value.

---

72. Fun With Surveys

When companies are considering new products or trying to find new ways to sell old products, they hire people to go out and talk to shoppers. Shoppers are questioned about products they like, don't like, and how they spend their money. The company uses this research to decide what products to manufacture, how to package their products, and how to advertise.

You can take surveys, too!

1. Suggest that your child conduct a survey to see if more people like chocolate bars with nuts or without.
2. On a large sheet of posterboard, draw two bar graphs. Draw lines every half inch all the way up the bars to make grids for marking answers to the survey.
3. Then buy one of each candy bar (for "testing," of course) and paste the wrappers on your poster, one beneath each bar.
4. Start the survey by asking your child which candy bar she likes best. Show her how to color in one block on the grid to record her vote.
5. Let her ask other family members and record their preferences. Explain that her job is to ask everyone who calls on the phone or comes to your house for the next week which candy bar they prefer.
6. At the end of the week, talk about the results. If you were going to sell chocolate bars to the people you know, and you had to choose plain or nuts, which would be best to sell? If you were going to invent a new chocolate bar, how would the results of this survey help you?

For more fun

Think of other surveys you could conduct: favorite breakfast foods, favorite fast-food restaurants, favorite movies, favorite pets. Then think of other ways to make graphs. A graph to show breakfast food preferences could be drawn like bowls of cereal. Each vote could be recorded by coloring a small circle representing a bite of cereal.

MoneySkills

✔When companies make decisions about new products, they do research to find out what shoppers like best.

✔Graphing responses to a survey helps us picture the results and understand them better.

✔My opinion is important to stores, businesses, and manufacturers.

PRODUCT SURVEY

Question:

_____

Product #1:   **Product #2:**

_____   _____

Record answers to your survey by coloring one block for each vote on the correct bar graph.

Results: _____

73. Conducting Taste Tests

When your child starts begging for the newest cereal advertised on TV, try this approach.

Store aisle research

1. When you go shopping, spend a little extra time in the cereal aisle. Find the cereal from TV and two similar cereals. Write down the price and weight of each. Show your child how to compare the cost per unit (usually cost per ounce).

2. Then ask questions: Which cereal looks best to you? What do you like about it? Is it the box or the prize inside? Is it the size or shape? Read the labels. Which cereal provides the best nutritional value?

Kitchen table research

1. Choose three similar cereals, including the one on TV, for a taste test. Invite the whole family to participate.

2. Make labels for "Cereal A," "Cereal B," and "Cereal C." On the back of each label where no one can see, write the name of the cereal. Tape the labels to the bowls.

3. Blindfold everyone so they can't see the color, size, or shape of the cereals. Pour a small amount of each cereal in a bowl. Mix up the bowls.

4. Let each person taste the three cereals and vote on the one they like best. Write down each person's response, but keep all votes secret.

5. Now reveal the results. Was the cereal from the TV ad the winner of the taste test? If so, maybe this is a good product to buy. If another brand wins, discuss what you have learned. What tactics are used on commercials to make us want to buy a particular product?

More testing

Buy a generic (or store brand) cake mix and a well-known brand. Bake both cakes and conduct a taste test. Can you tell the difference? Which one do you like best? Is the money you save by buying the store brand worth it? Other products you might test: puddings, peanut butter, hot chocolate mix.

MoneySkills

✔To find the unit price of a product, divide the price by the number of ounces in the box.

✔Color, size, shape, and packaging influence our buying decisions.

---

74. Classified Information

The daily newspaper is a great tool for teaching your child about money. He already knows how to find the comics and the sale papers for his favorite stores! But he also needs to know how to read and use classified ads.

Finding your way around

- Show your child the classified ad section of the paper. Explain that items for sale are listed in categories. Look at the directory (or index) for the classifieds that lists all the categories of things for sale.
- Play a game of guessing categories for items you might want to buy. You call out "bed." Your child says "furniture." You call out "guitar." Your child says "musical instruments."

Looking for bargains

1. When you are looking for a particular item to buy, put your child in charge of checking the classified ads each day. Show your child how to find the right section and how to read the ads. Ask him to mark with a highlighter the ads that look promising.

2. Write a list of the three most important questions to ask and let your older child make preliminary calls on the ads. Have your child write the information about each call on a 3 x 5 card.

3. Have your child listen while you make follow-up calls on the ads he has marked. Discuss what you like or don't like and make additional notes on your 3 x 5 cards.

4. After a few days, evaluate your research. What is the highest price you've found? What is the lowest? Which appears to be the best quality? How much can you save buying second-hand rather than new?

5. Pick the top three to five most promising prospects and take your child with you to see the items. On the way, talk about your criteria for quality and how you will negotiate "the deal." After you've made the purchase, thank your child for helping you find a good bargain.

MoneySkills

✔Buying second-hand is a good way to save money on items like furniture and cars.

✔With patience, we can usually find bargains in the classified ad section of the newspaper.

---

75. Menu Math

It is important that children relate math skills they learn in the classroom to daily living. Show your child how we use quick mental arithmetic to estimate costs when we read menus, price lists, and sale ads.

Mental math with take-out menus

1. Save take-out and home delivery menus from favorite local eating establishments. The next time you're in the mood to "order in," give your child the menus and a budget—perhaps $20—to feed the family.

2. She should first divide $20 by the number of people in the family to estimate the average amount each person's order may cost. (If there are four in the family, each person's order must be under $5.) Now look for items on the menu that are less than $5.

3. Consider ways to save money (sharing an order, buying what's on special, etc.). How much can you save if you don't buy drinks? Give your child a little incentive: Pay her to prepare the drinks at home!

4. Challenge your child to come up with two order combinations that will please the family and stay within the budget. Ask her to write down the orders, the cost of each item, and an estimate of the total. Explain how to estimate the sales tax as well as a tip that will be added to the bill.

5. Show her you appreciate her work by following her suggestions when you order. How close was her estimate to the actual total?

More to think about

1. Could you save money by preparing the same meal at home? While you are waiting for dinner to be delivered, show your child how to estimate how much it would cost to prepare your "order-in" meal at home. How much would you save?

2. Explain that the extra cost of the meal is what we pay to have someone cook for us. "Ordering in" saves time and work, but it costs more.

MoneySkills

✔When we read menus or price lists, we can use quick mental arithmetic to estimate our total bill.

✔Eating out usually costs more because we pay someone to cook for us.

---

76. First Wheels

A bicycle provides kids with cheap transportation and a lot of chances to learn responsibility with money.

Getting the best buy

1. Before you start bike shopping, have a talk with your child about the family budget and how much you can spend on a bike.
2. If you have limited funds, consider buying a used bike. Show your child how to read classified ads, shop garage sales, and look for good deals at second-hand stores.
3. If you are looking for a new bike, read the sale ads in the newspaper. Visit several stores together to see the bikes and compare prices. Don't forget to check discount stores and warehouse outlets.
4. Help your child set up a chart comparing prices and features of the bikes you're considering. Make a decision together about the best buy.

Basic maintenance saves money

1. When you get the bike home, show your child how to check tires, tighten the seat, lube the chain, and inspect regularly for loose nuts and bolts or signs of any parts needing repair.

2. Flat tires are inevitable on bikes. Have your child call the bike repair shop and find out what they charge to repair a flat. Then have him figure how much it costs to fix it himself.
3. Learning to repair a flat requires some practice and a strong desire to ride rather than walk. Always carefully inspect any work your child does on his bike before he rides it again.

Responsibility with bikes

Give your child a special place to park his bike and expect him to use only that spot. For repeat parking "violations," write a "ticket" and make him pay a "fine." Teach him to lock his bike every time he gets off, no matter where he is. If the bike is stolen because your child was careless, let him earn his own money for the next bike.

MoneySkills

✔Shoppers save money by checking at least 3 stores to find lowest prices and best quality.

✔We save money when we take good care of what we own.

---

77. Junk Mail

Instead of throwing away those sheets of discount stamps for magazine subscriptions you get in the mail, save them. Even "junk" mail can be used to teach kids about money!

How to buy magazines at discount

1. Ask your child to look at the magazine stamps you saved and select a magazine she would enjoy reading.
2. Go to the store together and buy a copy of that magazine from the newsstand. Give your child a few days to read and decide if this is a magazine she would like to receive each month.
3. Look for coupons in the magazine that offer discounts on new subscriptions. How much is a one-year subscription? Is it more or less than the discount offer you received in the mail? How much is the regular subscription rate with no discounts? How much will the magazine cost if you buy it each month at the newsstand?
4. Show your child how to make a chart comparing the four subscription rates. Explain how to divide the yearly subscription rate by the number of issues to determine the cost per month. Which offer gives you the lowest cost per month?
5. If you have decided to subscribe to the magazine, help your child fill out the subscription blank and mail it in. Explain that it will be several weeks before her first issue arrives.

To think about

1. Explain to your child that you use this same system of comparing prices when you subscribe to a new magazine. Show her a copy of your favorite magazine. How much does the magazine cost on the newsstand? How much do you save by having your own subscription?
2. Discuss the fact that this is only a true savings if you read the magazine and benefit from its information each month. If you never read the magazine, you have wasted your money anyway.

MoneySkills

✔We save money by looking for discounts on things we want to buy.

✔If we don't use things we buy, we have wasted our money.

---

78. TV: Facts and Other Messages

If your child watches a lot of TV, he sees hundreds of commercials every month, all designed to get him to buy, buy, buy. Help your child recognize ways TV makes us want to buy.

Just the facts, please

1. Ask your child to choose two of his favorite TV commercials about food. Watch them closely whenever they come on.
2. Then get a sheet of paper and divide it into two columns. Label the left column "Fact." Label the right column "Other Messages."
3. Under "Fact," list the real facts about the product that were mentioned or shown in the commercial. These might include information about size or color, price, or cooking and preparing information.
4. Under "Other Messages," list messages that may not be fact—such as someone's opinion, an exaggeration or a promise to make the consumer more loved, accepted or popular. Statements like, "Tastes better than your mom's," or "If you eat X you'll grow up to be strong/smart/beautiful," are examples of messages that aren't facts.
5. Which list is longest? Discuss the fact that most TV commercials sell us products by promising us love, security, and acceptance.
6. The next time you see those commercials, notice how the children are smiling, people are hugging, and everyone is happy. Scenes like this make us think of the product as something good for us. People don't realize they are buying products because they want to be loved. Why don't we just hug each other more instead of buying cookies?

Take the challenge!

When you see a commercial that makes big promises about a product, take it as a challenge. Try the test they show on TV at home. Does the product really do what they say in the commercial? If not, write a complaint letter to the company.

MoneySkills
✔Many messages in TV commercials are not based on facts about the product.
✔We should realize that TV commercials use special words, music, pictures, and props to make us want to buy.

---

79. The Ad Game

TV is not the only place children see ads. Magazines ads, newspapers ads, signs, and store displays are all part of everyday life. Make a game of identifying the sales techniques advertisers use to win our business.

Learning the "rules" of the game

Show your child three different magazines. Look through the magazines together and see if you can find examples of these kinds of ads:

1. The Happy Scene Ad: This type of ad shows families smiling, talking, hugging each other as they enjoy using a product. It implies that you will be happy if you buy that product or use that brand.
2. The Exciting Event Ad: Thess ads show sports events where everyone is excited and yelling and having a good time. It implies you will have a good time if you use a certain product.
3. The Hero Speaks Ad: This type of ad features a well-known sports hero, movie star, or famous person saying how much he or she likes a certain product. It implies you will be important or famous if you also use that product.
4. The New Improved Ad: This ad uses lots of words that tell us the product is new and improved, better than before, and ready to solve any problem. It implies a better product, but better compared to what?
5. The Special Information Ad: This ad uses words and numbers to make it sound like they have lots of proof their product is better than others. It implies that if you are smart, you will use the product.

Ask yourself these questions:

1. What is this ad trying to make us believe?
2. What details in the ad support the message?
3. Are there good reasons to buy this product?

MoneySkills

✔We can study the words and pictures used in advertising and understand how the ads make us want to buy.

✔Smart shoppers examine products closely to see if they are really as good as they are advertised.

---

80. Eating Out On a Budget

It's expensive to take the family out to eat. Show your child how to use proper "budget etiquette" when you eat out.

Ordering from a menu

1. Explain to your child that when families go out to eat, parents set the dollar limit on orders: "Tonight our limit is ... "

2. Open the menu and look at it together. Show your child how to read the left-hand column where the entrees are listed and the right-hand column where the prices are listed. What is the lowest-priced entree on the menu? What is the highest-priced entree? What is the price you see most often?

3. Which entrees can you order and stay within the budgeted amount? Are drinks extra? What about a salad? Explain how to round each item to the nearest dollar and add to see if you are staying within your limit.

4. If your child wants to choose an expensive item, is there something less expensive he likes just as well? Is there a smaller serving of the same entree?

5. As the orders are given, let children try to estimate the total bill. Instruct them to play this game quietly and do the adding in their heads. (Also, explain that it's OK to do this when the family is eating out, but *not* when we are entertaining guests.)

Checking the bill

1. When the bill arrives, read it together and check to see if it is correct. Congratulate the family for working together to stay within the budget!

2. Talk about why we leave tips at restaurants. Let your child help figure the tip. What is 10 percent of the bill? 15 percent? 20 percent?

MoneySkills
✔We use quick mental math to estimate how much we are spending before we order.
✔Always check your bill to see if it is correct.

---

81. Water Bills

Children today are very conscious of saving the earth and its resources. Ask your child to join you in a test to see how much of the earth's resources you use when you take a shower. Then see if you can save family resources by cutting back on the water bill.

Try an experiment

1. Set a one-gallon container in the shower. Ask your child to turn on the water for a normal shower.
2. Use a timer to see how long it takes to fill the one-gallon container with water. Now estimate how many gallons you use each minute you run the shower.
3. Let's see if you are right. Set a large trash can under the shower. Turn on the shower for exactly one minute. Use the one-gallon container to measure how much water you ran.

Make a chart

1. Now do some calculating. Ask your child to make a chart showing the family how much water is used for showers of various lengths: 5 min., 10 min., 15 min., etc.
2. If everyone in the family saved 10 gallons of water a day, how much water would you save in one week? How about in one month? How much in a year?

Look at the bill

Study your last water bill together. How many gallons did your family use? What was the total bill? How much did each gallon cost? How much money could you save if each person used 10 gallons less water each day?

Brainstorm together about ways to save water in the shower, in the kitchen, washing the car, etc. Offer a reward. If the water bill goes down, you'll put the money saved each month into a special account to be used for family outings or something the family wants to buy.

MoneySkills

✔ We have to pay for every gallon of water we use each month.

✔ We can lower our water bill if we all look for ways to save water.

✔ Money we save on utilities can be used for other things we want.

---

82. "Free" Pets

Sooner or later, all kids want pets. Before you accept that "free" puppy, help your child discover what it really costs to raise an animal. It may be worth it. Pets are a very good way to teach children over 8 or 9 years old about responsibility.

Investigate first

Adopting a pet into the family is an important event. Before you take the plunge, have your child do some reading and investigation. Go to the library. Contact local animal shelters or veterinarians for free booklets and information about the pet you are considering. Ask friends and relatives about their pets.

What will it cost?

1. Have your child make a list of things the pet will need and what they will cost:
   - Food, feeding bowls, collar and chain, bedding, a fenced yard, city tags and licenses.
   - Visits to the vet: shots, worming, check ups, sick visits
   - Grooming: shampoos, flea collars, flea sprays, yard and house sprays
2. Estimate the weekly cost of caring for your pet. Whose job will it be to pay the expenses of having a pet?

How much time?

Discuss the time involved in caring for a pet each week. Make a schedule for an average day of caring for the pet. Talk with your child about the job of caring for a pet and how he would feel about keeping the schedule.

Alternative pets

If a puppy is totally out of the question, how about considering a less-common alternative: snails, earthworms, crickets, ants, and hermit crabs. All of these are inexpensive, take little care, and can be quite educational.

> *MoneySkills*
> ✔When someone offers you something free, consider the hidden costs.
> ✔If we have a pet, it is our responsibility to have the money to take care of it properly.

83. The Young Collector

Children love to collect: stamps, baseball cards, coins, stickers, rocks, shells, books, action figures, posters, tapes, etc. Since building a collection takes money, your child will have a great incentive to save and manage his resources.

Supporting a hobby

1. Help your child find out what it costs to be a collector. Read books. Send off for catalogs. Talk to other people. Pick up price lists at craft stores and hobby shops.
2. Compare prices. Find ways to save money on supplies. Watch garage sales and local classified ads for hobby supplies.
3. Look for ways a hobby can support itself. Are there any built-in money-making possibilities?
4. Help your child think of extra jobs he might do around the house or neighborhood. You may want to help by giving something for the collection at birthdays and holidays.

Preserving your investment

Help your child see that each time he adds to his collection, he is investing in something that may one day be worth much more than he paid for it.

Help him find inexpensive ways to preserve and display his collection. Scrapbooks or old school notebooks are excellent for stickers, photos, baseball cards, and postcards. Inexpensive bulletin boards can be made of a large sheet of cardboard covered with burlap. An old tackle box or last year's lunch box is great for storing small parts, art supplies, and crafts. Watch garage sales for old picture frames, shelves, and display materials.

Becoming an expert

Check out books at the library. Go to free demonstrations, workshops, hobby and craft fairs, coin and baseball card conventions. Join clubs. Subscribe to magazines. Watch for newspaper articles. Start a special file folder for brochures, articles, handouts, instruction booklets, and information on classes, clubs, and resources.

MoneySkills
✔Well-preserved collections often become valuable because they are rare.
✔I can find ways to save money and earn money for my hobbies.

---

84. Volunteer as a Family

Here's a way to combat the "me, me, me/buy, buy, buy" syndrome of the December holidays: volunteer to help a needy family. Your church, synagogue, or community social service agency can help you get started with ideas on how to help.

Financing your project

1. Start a tradition of setting aside 10 percent of your gift-buying budget to help a needy family.
2. Your child may contribute money she has been collecting in the Sharing Bank (see Activity 23).
3. Make the money you have budgeted for this project spread as far as you can. Use coupons, shop sales, go to thrift shops, and watch for giveaways you could use as stocking stuffers.
4. Tell other relatives or friends about your project. They may have food, clothing, or used toys to contribute.

Divide up the work

1. First make a list of things that need to be done. Then allow family members to volunteer for the various jobs.
2. Your child can look through her closet and shelves for good toys, books, and clothes she has outgrown. She can also help bake cookies, make small gifts, and help shop for food baskets.
3. Spend an evening checking over everything, making sure toys still work, clothes are clean and mended, and there is a gift for each person in your adopted family. Let your child help wrap gifts and box the food and clothes.
4. Go as a family to deliver your gifts. Afterward, talk about how fortunate you are to be able to help others. Enjoy hot chocolate and cookies together when you get home.

MoneySkills

✔It's a good thing to share with people who are less fortunate.

✔It is my responsibility to give as well as receive at holidays.

---

85. A Day for Giving

Children should be involved in gift giving as well as gift receiving at Christmas and Hanukkah. Help your child prepare small gifts for each member of the family. You'll know it's been worth the time when you hear your child saying, "I can't wait to see you open your gift!" (Instead of the usual, "When can I open my presents?")

Gifts of time rather than money

1. Challenge your family to find gifts that people love to receive, cost no money, and can't be "boxed."
   - Examples for children: play ball with my brother for one hour, take my sister's turn helping with dishes for one week, wash the car for my parents, give the dog a bath.
   - Examples for parents: go bike riding with you for one hour, read an extra 10 minutes every night before bed this week, let you use my nail polish.
2. Provide colored paper, envelopes, markers, glitter, and art supplies to make gift "coupons" or "certificates."
3. Encourage your child to make small gifts from things you find around the house. Examples: a decorated juice can becomes a pencil holder; cookie cutters, scraps of felt and trim become tree ornaments; drapery rings become mini-picture frames. Magazines and newspapers are full of ideas in November and December. Or visit the library for books on children's crafts.
4. Help your child disguise her gifts in gigantic boxes, unusual hiding places, and creative wraps. It's all part of the fun of giving!

Being first to GIVE

Start a family tradition when your children are young that stresses the "giving" aspect of holidays. "We're going to see who is first to *give* a gift this year." Draw numbers to see who gets to be first to give out his gifts. Let everyone watch as each gift is opened. Take time to express appreciation to the giver. Then another family member may take his turn giving his gifts.

MoneySkills

✔The price of a gift is not as important as the love it expresses.

✔Even if I don't have a lot of money to spend, I can find ways to give.

Activities That Teach Money *Smarts*

Many of the decisions your 9- to 12-year-old will make with money in the next few years will require moral and ethical value judgments. Family talks help children set standards about priorities so they will be prepared to make correct decisions.

Tough Questions

Take turns making up tough questions to ask each other or the whole family. Everyone has to be honest, and there should be no criticism of a family member for his or her answer. These sample questions represent common dilemmas your child is likely to face:

1. What if you found a wallet with $100 in it and an ID that gives the owner's address?
2. What if the checker at the grocery store made a mistake and charged you $5 for an item that costs $2? What if she charged you $2 for something that costs $5?
3. What if you saw someone shoplifting? What if you saw one of your friends shoplifting?
4. What if you were standing in line to make a phone call and the person in front of you left his change in the phone?
5. What if a restaurant had a box on the counter for customers to make their own change and pay their own bills? Would it work, or would people steal from the box?
6. What if the bank put $10 in your account by mistake? What if the bank put $1,000 in your account by mistake?
7. What if you were small for your age and could trick people into letting you into the movies for child prices?

Right decisions

These talks should be in-depth discussions, not parental lectures. Every person should have a chance to state his views on the subject. Children should be respected as individuals who have valuable ideas.

Talking about these situations in advance will help children make right decisions. If you disagree with a child's answer, suggest an alternate solution or ask, "Have you thought of...?" Keep the conversation moving and the questions popping. Listen to the dilemmas your child presents. You may learn a great deal about the world your child faces every day.

86. Investigating Banks

If your child does not have a savings account yet, it's time to help her get one started. Put her in charge of investigating several banks and choosing the one she likes best.

Visiting banks

1. Ask your child to make a list of questions she has about opening a savings account at a bank.
2. Then choose several banks in your community to visit. Take your checklist along and be sure to get information about each point. Talk to a customer service representative, make notes, collect brochures and, if possible, take a tour of the bank.
3. If you are a credit union member, take your child to the credit union also. Explain how credit unions are like banks and how they are different.
4. Review what you saw and learned during your visits. Consider which bank is most convenient, offers the best services, pays the highest interest, and is most friendly to children.

Opening your account

When you are ready to open the account, go to the bank together. Remember to take your child's Social Security number with you. Let your child fill out the application and answer the questions. Make this a joint account, but have the statements addressed to your child. Before you leave, pick up a supply of deposit slips and withdrawal forms.

Once home, help your child find a safe place to keep her passbook, deposit slips, and receipts. Talk about what this money will be used for and any rules she will be expected to follow about withdrawals.

Savings goals

While enthusiasm is high, encourage your child to set goals for making regular deposits to her account. Give your child a special notebook. Ask her to write three goals that involve saving money. Under each goal ask her to write two things she needs to do to achieve that goal. Then give her a calendar and let her set dates for accomplishing the goals she has set.

MoneySkills

✔Money "grows" when we keep it in a savings account and make regular deposits.

✔We are more likely to accomplish financial goals if we write them down.

---

87. The Magic of Compounding

Something magic happens in savings accounts. As your money earns interest and the account grows larger, it earns more interest until eventually your account has doubled. The principle of compound interest gives kids (and adults!) some exciting reasons to start a savings program.

Explaining compound interest

1. Sit together at the kitchen table with pencil and paper. Show your child that if he puts $10 in the bank and earns 5 percent interest, he will have $10.50 at the end of the year. How much in 10 years?

2. Your child may guess 10 times 50 cents, or $5 interest. Wrong. If you leave that interest in the account and let it draw interest *too*, you will have $16.30 at the end of 10 years. This is "compounding interest."

3. Most people don't put just $10 in their accounts. Suppose you make regular deposits to that account. How much will $100 become in 10 years? ($163.) What about $1,000? ($1,630.)

4. How long do you think it will take for your first $10 deposit to double? We could figure this out mathematically, but bankers use a special rule they call "the rule of 72."

Rule of 72

If you divide 72 by the rate of interest, you will know the number of years it takes for your money to double.

- Savings at 5 percent interest doubles in 14.4 years.
- Savings at 9 percent interest doubles in 8 years.

An illustration of compounding

Now get out the family checkerboard and a jar of pennies. Place one penny on the first square. Ask your child to put two pennies on the next square. Then put four pennies on the third square. Keep doubling: 8 pennies, 16 pennies, 32 pennies, 64 pennies, 128 pennies. Look what happens when money doubles again and again! How many pennies would it take to complete every square on the board? Millions! Now you understand the "magic" of compounding interest!

MoneySkills

✔Compound interest makes our money grow faster because the interest earns interest.

✔If I divide 72 by the yearly rate of interest, I can find out the number of years it will take for my money to double.

Credit Application

Name: _____ Age: _____

Address: _____

Phone: _____ School: _____

Sources of income: Money you owe:
1.   1.

2.   2.

3.   3.

People who have loaned you money before:

1.

2.

Amount you wish to borrow: _____

What the money will be used for:_____
_____

Your plans for repaying the loan:_____
_____

Date loan will be paid:_____

Approved   ❑

Not approved   ❑

Borrower: _____

Loan officer: _____

88. The Bank of Mom

Children in grade school are too young to need a checking account, but they are not to young to start learning how one works. Use this game to show your child how to manage a checking account.

Here's how it works

1. Set up a banking system with your kids, complete with receipt books, checkbooks, and deposit slips. Use the sample checks in this book or give kids the job of making the banking forms you'll need on 3 x 5 cards.

2. Let the kids deposit their allowances with you and write "checks" against the Bank of Mom when they want to spend money.

3. Show kids how to make a "check register" and keep a running balance of their account. Don't forget, it's your job as the banker to bounce checks for insufficient funds.

4. To slow down a heavy spender, require two days notice for a withdrawal. To encourage saving, offer to pay interest on what stays in the bank for at least one week.

Loan policy

Set limits about how often loans can be made—no more than once a week and if you borrow this week, there will be no borrowing next week.

Require borrowers to fill out a "credit application" and sign a contract. Charge a small interest rate on the unpaid balance.

MoneySkills

✔To write checks there has to be real money in my checking account.

✔I must always know how much money is in my checking account so I don't make a mistake and write a check for too much.

✔Credit is a privilege I earn by showing I can be responsible to pay money back on time.

---

89. A Money Diary

The Money Diary is a very effective tool for teaching kids to be responsible with money. One parent says her college-age daughter still uses this system. It's no longer required by her parents, but it works.

Getting started

1. Tell your child ahead of time that you are planning something very special for her birthday to celebrate "growing up."
2. Set a time and place for this event so both parents, and perhaps even other family members, can be present.
3. Present your child with a beautifully wrapped box. Inside is a special log book for recording her financial transactions. Call it her money diary.
4. At that time your child is to empty her pockets, count all the money in her piggy bank, look for money laying around her room, and give an account of her total financial worth.
5. Help your child label the columns on the first page of the diary: Date, Paid To/Received From, For What, Amount, Balance. Show her how to record her total cash on hand as the beginning balance of her financial record.
6. Explain that from now on she will be be able to write down every cent she spends each day, enter the date, what the money was spent on, and the amount. If she earns money or adds to her wealth, she is to enter that in her book. She is to keep a running balance. At the end of each week, she counts all her money again to see if the books balance.

The value of the money diary

The money diary is a long-term system put into place now and used until your child graduates from high school. There will be times when your child will gripe about the diary. But as a parent you know that it takes a lot of short-term inconveniences to teach kids long-term values.

MoneySkills

✔Smart money managers always know how much money they have and where every penny is spent.

✔Keeping a money diary helps me know when I am spending too much money on things that don't last.

✔When I know how I spend money, I can plan my spending and make better decisions.

---

90. The Allowance Review

One of the biggest mistakes parents make with allowances is not giving enough. As your child grows older, you will want to review his needs and make adjustments to his allowance. Keep in mind the purpose of the allowance is to give your child enough money to practice making spending decisions, but not enough to be frivolous. Also, keep in mind that a 9- to 12-year-old is old enough to earn some of his money for extra expenses.

Consider goals

1. Ask your child to make a list of the five most important things he would like to do with his allowance. Then ask him to estimate how much of his allowance he would spend on each item.
2. Look over the list together and ask your child to explain what he has written. Listen carefully. A kid who wants to invest in baseball cards or buy computer software is ready for a larger allowance than a kid whose only goal is to buy candy at the baseball game.
3. If your child is requesting a hefty raise, ask him to submit a written "proposal" or sample budget showing his income and expenses for an ideal week.
4. Take some time to think about your own goals for teaching your child to save, budget, and contribute to charity. And consider the overall family financial picture. Then determine how much allowance your child will receive.

Encourage saving first

Here's a great way to make your child feel grown up, teach him about banking, and encourage him to save. Start paying his allowance by check. This will call for a trip to the bank to cash the check. He will learn how to endorse the check and how to take it to the teller and ask for cash. It is also the perfect opportunity for him to deposit his 10 percent savings into his passbook account—*before* he ever leaves the bank, enters a store, and is tempted to spend it all.

MoneySkills

✔Smart money managers base their spending plans on goals.

✔As I grow older and receive a larger allowance, I have a greater responsibility to manage money wisely.

---

91. A Personal Spending Plan

To many of us, "budget" is a dirty word. It sounds too much like "diet" (something else we all hate!). Budgets and diets make us feel deprived. If you feel this way, try using the words "spending plan" instead of budget. Then start early teaching your child to appreciate the value of a wise spending plan.

Understanding income and expenses

1. Sit down at the kitchen table with your child. Explain that you are going to show her a "secret" formula for managing money that many people never discover.

2. Show your child two sheets of construction paper, each a different color. Ask her to write "Income" at the top of one and "Expenses" at the top of the other.

3. Explain that Income is all the money that "comes in" to your possession. On a sheet of notebook paper, have your child list all her possible sources of income: allowance, gifts, odd jobs, finding money, winning contests, investment income, etc.

4. Expenses are all the ways you spend money or the ways money "goes out" of your possession. On another sheet of notebook paper, have your child list all the ways she spends money. Include the money she sets aside for saving and charity.

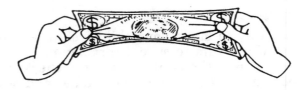

Fixed or flexible?

5. Look at your lists of Income and Expenses. Put a star by the items on each list that occur weekly and are usually for the same amount. These are "fixed" expenses and income. Those that occur irregularly are "flexible" expenses and income.

6. Fold the sheets of construction paper labeled Income and Expenses in half. Label the top halves "Fixed." Label the bottom halves "Flexible."

7. Now have your child copy her lists of Income and Expenses to the sheets of construction paper you've prepared, fixed at the top, flexible at the bottom. Leave at least 1 inch between each item.

8. Use a pencil to write amounts beside each entry for Income and Expenses. What is the total of your Fixed Income? What is the total of your Fixed Expenses? How much money will you have left over when your Fixed Expenses are paid?

9. Now ask your child to total her Flexible Expenses. Is there enough money left in Fixed Income to cover all the Flexible Expenses? Probably not! What do you think we can do?

Making choices

10. When your *income* is not enough to balance your *out*-go (Expenses), you have two choices: 1) earn more money, or 2) spend less money. Talk about your options.

11. Cut the Flexible Expenses apart in strips and let your child arrange them in order of importance. Can you decrease the amount you plan to spend on some of the expenses? Which expenses might be delayed? Which ones could be taken off the list entirely?

12. Look at the Flexible Income list. Can you add more ways to earn extra money? Cut the Flexible Income list into strips. Can you match ways to earn extra money with some of the flexible expenses?

13. Show your child how to shift money from one item to the next and adjust the amounts until the budget balances. But remember, your child needs to make the decisions.

Follow up

14. When the spending plan is balanced, glue the finished "budget" on a piece of posterboard and hang it in your child's room.

15. On allowance day, show your child how to divide her money into different envelopes or banks (see Activities 23 and 52) for each of the Fixed Expenses in her spending plan.

16. At the end of each week, show your child how to look at her money diary (*MoneySkill* 89) and add up what she actually spent on each Fixed and Flexible Expense. Use the chart on the following page to evaluate your spending for the week. Did you go over your budget? Did you stay under your budget? Any extra you have left over each week is called your "surplus." What will you do with it?

17. Expect your child to adjust her spending plan regularly. Perhaps she will want to start a notebook for her spending plans as she becomes more skilled at financial planning.

MoneySkills

✔A budget is a careful plan for spending and saving the money that we earn or receive.

✔When Income is not enough to balance Expenses, we can choose to earn more money or find ways to spend less money.

✔Fixed Expenses are regular expenses for necessities. Flexible Expenses are occasional expenses for things we could usually do without.

MY SPENDING PLAN

	Week 1		Week 2	
	Planned	Spent	Planned	Spent
Fixed Expenses:				
Flexible Expenses:				
Totals:				

Use this chart to see how well you stayed on your spending plan.

92. Teamwork

Every member of the family should have jobs or chores they do regularly to help around the house. These are things we do just because we live here and we are a family. We do not get paid.

Kids contribute their labor more willingly when they know their contribution really helps—that it really makes a difference. Let your child know he is a valuable member of the team.

Promote your team!

Start a dinner discussion about times you've worked together to get things done. Good examples might be the garage sale you had last summer, the meal you cooked tonight, or the flowerbeds you planted last month. Talk about how each person did a small part in order to get a big job accomplished. Stress that the job couldn't have been done without each person's help.

Teamwork means more money for the family to spend

1. Make a list of the chores family members do around the house without being paid. Beside each, write the amount you would have to pay someone else to do the work.
2. Choose a day when the family has worked well together and everyone deserves a pat on the back. Then show your list and congratulate each person for their valuable contributions to the family.
3. When your child helps paint his room or rakes the yard so you don't have to hire someone, tell him how much money his work is saving the family.

When the team wins, everyone shares the prize!

1. Plan ways to reward the family for their hard work. It doesn't have to be something that costs a lot of money. Plan a picnic, visit the zoo, or barbecue in the backyard.
2. To make the point even more clear you might say, "Annie saved us so much money this week, we can all go out to a movie!"

MoneySkills

✔Working together as a team helps our family save time and get more done.

✔Money we save by doing our own work can be used for other things we want or need.

---

93. Extra Jobs

Working at home for extra money is your child's first experience at a real job, and it's a great way to prepare him to be self sufficient. He doesn't have to know it was your intention to make his allowance small enough that he would have an incentive to do extra work. The important thing is that he learns to take initiative in managing his financial situation. Earning money for special jobs at home or in the neighborhood gives kids a greater sense of freedom and control over their personal finances.

Use stick-on notes

1. If you have closets, cabinets, or drawers that need to be cleaned, use stick-on notes to label them with messages like, "Clean by Saturday for 50 cents." (For your own record, make a list of cabinets you labeled and how much each was worth.)
2. Make sure your child understands the steps for cleaning a cabinet. First, remove everything. Then wash the cabinet and put in new shelf paper if necessary. Sort and organize the contents, removing things that do not belong, and put everything back. (Label the shelves ahead of time to help kids get things where you can find them again.)

Post a list

1. Make a list of about 10 extra jobs around your house—not regular chores—that you would be willing to pay someone to do.
2. Beside each one, list how much you will pay. This will be determined by the age and abilities of your child, where you live, and the family income.
3. Post the list on the refrigerator or family bulletin board. Explain to your child that it is up to him to choose a job and do the work if he wants to earn the money. Update your list often.
4. Your child will soon discover he can do these same jobs for a neighbor and get paid for the experience he gained at home.

MoneySkills

✔When I need extra money, I can look for extra jobs to do around the house or neighborhood.

✔The experience I get working at home prepares me to get jobs in the neighborhood.

---

94. A Matching Grants Program

Children in the upper grades are capable of setting goals and saving money for longer periods of time. They like to work on large goals like money for camp, family vacation, the newest video game system, a computer, a new bike, or a leather jacket.

When your child sets a high saving goal or is working for something that costs a lot of money, she will need encouragement.

Why a matching grants program?

1. Parents should not feel obligated to get children everything they want. If you just got through spending $300 for your child to go to summer camp or $500 for school clothes, it is ridiculous for you to feel guilty for not buying your child a new skateboard or a designer handbag. Encourage your child to earn or save the money for what she wants.

2. Most families today operate on a very tight budget. Sometimes the high-ticket items our kids want are things we would like for them to have—a computer, a musical instrument, sports or physical fitness equipment. If this is the case, consider offering to save along with your child, matching her savings dollar for dollar. This is an excellent way to inspire a youngster to stay focused on a long-term goal.

Setting up a matching grants program

1. Agree on what you are saving for, its price, and its intended use.
2. Set a time limit and decide where the money will be kept.
3. Sign a contract together stating these terms, and put it up where your child can see it every day.
4. Keep a record of your progress toward the goal at the bottom of the contract.

Another way to inspire saving

Offer to contribute something that compliments your child's goal. If she buys the skirt and jacket, you buy the shoes. If he buys the skateboard, you buy the kneepads.

MoneySkills

✔There is almost no limit to the savings goals I can set and meet if I am willing to work.

✔To stay on track toward meeting my goal, I need to think about my goal every day and keep a record of my progress.

---

95. Junior Investors

It's never too early to help your child become an investor. Consider giving several shares of stock to your child for a birthday present. Watch the stock grow and your child's interest in the stock market zoom!

What are the long-term benefits?

1. Your child begins to see herself as a junior partner in the economy.
2. Ownership helps kids develop a strong interest in the company they "own," and they'll enjoy following the daily stock reports.
3. Ownership motivates kids to learn what it takes to make a business successful or more profitable.
4. Your child could have a nice stock portfolio by the time she is 12.

Watching the stock market together

1. Help your child understand how to read the financial pages to see how much her stock goes up or down each day. Make a graph showing the fluctuation of the price of a share of stock. How much is your stock worth today? If you sold today, what profit or loss would you make on your investment?
2. Choose one or two other stocks to follow daily. For example, kids think it's fun to watch the stock for the companies where their parents or other relatives work.
3. Go to the library together and look for books that have pictures of the New York Stock Exchange trading floor action. Talk about how real people actually trade the stock, shouting out bids and making deals right on the spot.
4. Explain to your child that a stockbroker is someone who helps you buy and sell stock. Take your child with you to visit your stockbroker. If your child is highly interested in investing, consider opening a custodial account.
5. Watch for interesting newspaper articles about the stock market that you can share with your child. Explain that fluctuations and even wild swings in the market are normal and to be expected from time to time. Talk about how some people try to predict upswings and downswings by watching "economic indicators."

Play a stock market game

1. Give each person in the family $500 or $1,000 in play money to "buy" stocks.

2. One person is appointed broker, and it is his or her job to oversee the stock purchases, help each person keep track of their earnings, and make change from the "bank."
3. Players read the financial pages daily to check on their stock, discuss strategies with their broker, and buy and sell stock as they feel appropriate.
4. Whoever earns the most on their investments at the end of one month is declared the winner.

MoneySkills

✔We buy stock in companies we think will grow and make a profit.

✔I can read the stock market reports every day and see if the price on my stock goes up or down.

✔If the price of my stock goes higher than I paid, I can choose to sell my stock and make a profit.

---

96. Considering Careers

As your child gets older and starts looking at career possibilities, he will enjoy hearing how others selected their careers. You can help your child gather information from people you are around every day.

Interview friends

1. Think about people you know and the work they do. Help your child make a list of family members, friends, and neighbors and what they do for a living.
2. Are there any unusual careers on your list? Which jobs sound like something you'd like to know more about?
3. Arrange for your child to visit with several of these friends. Plan ahead and make a list of questions to ask this person:

   - How did you choose this career?
   - How did you get started?
   - What kind of training did you need?
   - Have there been problems to overcome in your career?

- What is it about this job that you like?
- What is the starting pay for someone in your career?
- What is top pay for someone experienced in your field?
- Do you have any advice for me?

4. Encourage your child to ask interesting people he meets these same questions.

Watch the papers

Collect pictures and articles about people with careers that might interest your child. What does the article tell you about how this person got started, his background, education, or obstacles he may have overcome? Do you think this person is happy with his work? Is he able to support himself adequately? If you were this person, what would you do differently? What would you do the same? After discussing an article, you may want to visit the library for more information about the career. Do you know someone else in this profession that your child could interview?

MoneySkills

✔I can start now investigating careers and thinking about the kind of job I would like.

✔Making money is only one thing to consider about a job.

---

97. Paying Bills

Children usually have no idea of daily living costs. They may not even realize that things like electricity and water cost money. This activity is a good way to talk to your child about "bills."

A guessing game

1. Make a list of your household bills. List the name of the bill on the left and put the amount on the far right.
2. Fold the sheet in half lengthwise and make a game out of letting your child guess how much each item costs. Write the child's guess in pencil next to the bill.
3. Unfold the sheet and compare the answers. Talk about how your family paycheck pays for all these things each month.

Responsibility with bills

1. Show your child what your bills look like. Talk about how the utility company allows you to use their service during the month with the understanding that you will pay what you owe at the end of the month. Talk about the responsibility you have to pay your bills on time and how good it feels to know you have honored your part of the agreement.
2. Change a paycheck into cash. Have your child watch as you put the money in separate piles for paying the bills. Then show your child how much is left for other things.

An energy audit

1. Explain that you will have more money for other things if the family can find ways to cut down on bills.
2. Appoint your child "energy auditor" for the day. Ask her to observe the family closely and make a list of ways you waste money on utilities.
3. Then ask your child to propose money saving solutions.

MoneySkills
✔Our monthly bills for water, gas, electricity, phone, etc., all have to be paid out of the family paycheck.
✔It is our responsibility to pay our bills on time each month.
✔If we save money on the monthly bills, we can spend more money for other things.

---

98. The Family That Earns Together

From time to time, every family wants to buy things that aren't in the budget. Why not earn the money together! Working toward a common financial goal gives kids a good example of how to start their own money making enterprises. Not only do they learn *how* to make money, they learn they really *can* make money!

Setting a specific goal

What is it your family wants? It may be a trampoline, a new computer, or a weekend trip. Have a meeting to discuss the project. Bring ads, sales brochures, prices, and supporting information to share. Then state your goal in writing, describing what you are working toward and how much money you need. Let each person read and sign the agreement.

Working together

You may have a family garage sale, collect aluminum cans, recycle newspaper, sell baked goods at the fair, or sell the old baby bed in the attic. Whatever projects you choose, do them together with each family member doing a specific part of the job.

Open a separate savings account for the money you earn toward the family goal. Each time you make a deposit, write details in a notebook: the date, how the money was earned or saved, and the amount. Make a chart to track your progress and post the chart where everyone can see it.

Additional ways to add to the fund

1. Have everyone in the family make a habit of throwing all the pennies and nickels in pockets and purses into a jar on the kitchen counter at the end of each day.
2. See how much lost money you can find. Watch for coins on the street, under the bed, in the couch, or left in pay phones.
3. Take your own snacks when you go places. Put the money you save in the account for your special project.
4. Become avid coupon clippers. Designate half the money you get back on coupons as money for your special project.

> *MoneySkills*
> ✔When we work together, our family can set and reach financial goals.
> ✔When I need extra money for something, I can find ways to earn it.
> ✔Saving small amounts of money adds up to large amounts of money.

99. Recycling for Cash

It takes very little time to drop a can in a sack or put newspaper in a box. Yet recycling projects teach your child to protect the environment, to use resources wisely, and...you can make a profit turning trash into cash!

How much can you earn?

1. The four most commonly recycled products are aluminum, newspaper, plastics, and glass. Ask your child how much he thinks he might earn each month by recycling these products.

2. Help your child find phone numbers for recycling centers in your community. Then have him call each center and find out what products they take and how much they pay per pound.

3. Show your child how to make a chart showing the local recycling centers and the prices they pay for aluminum, newspaper, plastics, and glass. Which center has the best prices?

4. Save up enough aluminum cans, newspaper, plastic jugs, and empty glass jars to make 1 lb. each. Give your child four paper sacks and a kitchen scale. Ask him to make a 1 lb. sack of each recyclable product.

5. How much is each sack worth? Ask your child to write the best price he found on the front of each sack. "Look what we can earn by saving things we throw away!"

Setting up a recycling system

Many families don't recycle because it's messy. Ask your child to help you find a way to solve this problem without spending money. Here are some suggestions:

- Use scrap lumber to build a recycling bin.
- Use cardboard boxes.
- Use 5 gallon buckets usually thrown away by carpenters, painters, or ice-cream stores.

If your child is earning the money from your recycling project, it should be his job to keep it clean and organized.

MoneySkills

✔People who care about the environment and our earth's resources save things that can be recycled.

✔Small change adds up to big bucks when you recycle.

---

100. Club Fundraisers

Sooner or later your child will be part of a fundraiser. When it's your child's turn to sell cookies, candy, candles, or magazine subscriptions, here's how to help.

Planning a sales talk

The hardest part about going out to sell candy is knowing what to say. This scares kids. So help your child work out a short speech which includes:

- An introduction of himself and his organization
- Why the group is trying to earn money
- Information about what he is selling
- How the product benefits customers
- The price
- A statement that asks the customer to buy now

Encourage your child to practice her sales talk at home, perhaps in front of a mirror or with a tape recorder. Coach your child to speak clearly, look the customer in the eye, and emphasize the benefits of her product.

Going out to sell

Be your child's first customer. Buy some candy and make sure she knows how to fill out the paper work. Then help your child make a list of people she knows who might want to buy candy. Call these your "target" customers. Choose the person on your list who is most likely to buy and go there first. Once your child gets a little success, she will have confidence to approach others on the list. If your child is going door to door, establish a clear set of safety guidelines. Accompany your child or have your child team up with a friend to go selling.

Overcoming discouragement

Why do people say no? It's usually because they bought from someone else, they're busy, they're on a diet, or they don't have the money. Experienced sales people say you have to ask 10 people to get one to say yes. Talk about what to do when people say no and how to keep on going until you find someone who says yes.

MoneySkills

✔A good sales talk tells the customer how he or she will benefit from the product.

✔Smart sales people pick customers who are most likely to say yes and ask them first.

---

101. Encouraging Young Entrepreneurs

After your child has gotten some work experience doing odd jobs for parents and neighbors, he may want to start a business. It will be well worth your time to help him get started. Running a business teaches kids to set goals, organize plans, manage resources, work within a budget, and be responsible with time and money.

Choosing a business idea

1. Take a walk through your neighborhood. Look for people who need help getting things done. Make an "opportunity list": cars to wash, gardens to weed, hedges to trim, fences to paint, pets to groom, errands to run, and moms that need baby-sitters.

2. Help your child make a list of jobs he knows how to do (things he has probably been doing at home) and could offer to do for pay. How many things on this list match with things on your opportunity list?

3. Give your child a copy of the book *Fast Cash for Kids* (Career Press, 1991) which my husband and I wrote for young entrepreneurs. In it, you'll find complete instructions for 101 businesses your child can start today.

4. Encourage your child to choose something that he likes to do. If he's having a good time, he will be able to stick with it longer and so will you.

5. If you have questions about taxes, permits, or licenses required in your city, call the local Chamber of Commerce.

Getting customers

When your child has settled on a business idea, help him think of a name for his business and ways to get customers:

1. Help him make a flier advertising that he is available for work. The flier should list jobs he is willing to do, for what prices, and how he can be contacted.

2. Then have your child make a list of people who are most likely to hire him. These are the people to contact first.

3. Deliver the fliers to the people on your list, then to all the houses on your street, and put some up at the nearest grocery store or laundromat.

4. If the flier doesn't bring customers on the first day, remind your child that neighbors will be thinking of him when they have a job to do.

5. In a few days, have your child phone or visit each person on his list of most likely customers to introduce his business and to offer a short free demonstration of his work. It won't be long before he gets his first job!

Guidelines to remember

1. Be firm about setting limits on how much time your child can spend working, especially during school months.

2. Before your child starts a job, make sure he is clear about how to do the job and what is expected of him.

3. Teach your child basic safety rules for tools and lawn equipment, household cleaners, babysitting, and, especially, traveling in the neighborhood.

4. Supervise your child's work. Expect him to give his best, be proud of his work, deal honestly, and always keep his word.

5. Coach your child on how to ask for the agreed-upon pay when the job is done. Teach your child to speak up for himself if someone tries to rip him off.

6. Don't be worried if your child wants to quit the business he started last week and start a new one this week. Kids this age jump from one project to another because they are in the process of discovering their talents and interests.

7. Help your child set up a record-keeping system to keep track of all income and expenses. Use the shoebox record-keeping system described in the book *Fast Cash for Kids*.

8. Encourage your child to keep a spiral notebook with customer's names, addresses, and phone numbers and notes about the jobs he does for each.

MoneySkills

✔I may be too young to get a real job, but I'm not too young to start my own business.

✔I should choose a business idea that I will enjoy.

✔To make my business a success, I must do good work and be dependable.

For More Information

Ancient coins

The history of coins goes back at least 2,700 years. This free booklet shows pictures of ancient coins and tells a brief history of each. Request "Coins of the Ancient Mediterranean World" from: Public Information Dept., Federal Reserve Bank of Philadelphia, P.O. Box 66, Philadelphia, PA 19105-0066

Money in the thirteen colonies

A shortage of money was a problem for early American settlers. This free booklet shows pictures of coins used in the 1700s and 1800s and tells a brief history of our first coins. Request "Money in Colonial Times" from: Public Information Dept., Federal Reserve Bank of Philadelphia, P.O. Box 66, Philadelphia, PA 19105-0066

Understanding banking

This free comic book tells the story of the island of Mazuma and how they invented money. Introduces basic concepts of bartering, money as a medium of exchange, and banking. Request "Once Upon a Dime" from: Federal Reserve Bank of New York, Public Information Dept., 33 Liberty St., New York, NY 10045

Mutilated money?

This free pamphlet answers question of what happens to money when it is worn out, burned, or mutilated. Request "Fedpoints 11: Currency Processing and Destruction" from: Federal Reserve Bank of New York, Public Information Dept., 33 Liberty St., New York, NY 10045

Story of checks

How checking accounts work, how checks are processed, and how to write a check are covered in this free comic book. Request "The Story of Checks and Electronic Payments" from: Federal Reserve Bank of New York, Public Information Dept., 33 Liberty St., New York, NY 10045

Compounding interest

An explanation of how interest rates are calculated. May be a little advanced for grade school, but has tables showing how compounding interest makes $1 grow each year. Request "The Arithmetic of Interest Rates," free from: Federal Reserve Bank of New York, Public Information Dept., 33 Liberty St., New York, NY 10045

What is a savings bond?

Three publications help answer that question. Request "U.S. Savings Bonds Buyers Guide," "The Savings Bond Question and Answer Book," and "U.S. Savings Bonds: Now Tax-Free for Education." Write to: Office of Public Affairs, U.S. Savings Bond Division, Dept. of the Treasury, Washington, DC 20226

Buying savings bonds

Receive a free book that tells all about savings bonds and shows color reproductions of old savings bond posters. Request "U.S. Savings Bonds" from: Federal Reserve Bank of Dallas, Public Affairs Dept., Station K, Dallas, TX 75222

Consumer protection laws

There are federal and state laws that protect consumers from unfair or dishonest business practices. Your child may receive a free pamphlet entitled "Kids are Consumers Too!" by writing to: Commonwealth of Massachusetts, Executive Office of Consumer Affairs, One Ashburton Place, Boston, MA 02108

Understanding credit

This comic book about consumer credit is available in either Spanish or English. Request "Story of Consumer Credit (English)" or "Story of Consumer Credit (Spanish)" from: Federal Reserve Bank of New York, Public Information Dept., 33 Liberty St., New York, NY 10045

Let's trade

Receive a comic book that explains the basics of foreign trade. Request "The Story of Foreign Trade and Exchange" from: Federal Reserve Bank of New York, Public Information Dept., 33 Liberty St., New York, NY 10045

Understanding nutrition labeling

To receive a free brochure that explains nutrition labeling printed on packaged foods, request "Nutrition Labeling: What Is It?" from: Kellogg Company, Food and Nutrition Communications, P.O. Box 3447, Dept. K-1, Battle Creek, MI 49016-3447

Recycling pays

For free helps and hints on recycling aluminum cans write to: Jenny Day, Can Manufacturers Institute, 1625 Massachusetts Ave., NW, Washington, DC 20036

Play clay recipe

You can make gifts, holiday decorations, and jewelry from homemade play clay. For easy directions, request the pamphlet "How to Make Play Clay" from: "Play Clay", Arm & Hammer Division, Church & Dwight Co., Inc., P.O. Box 7648, Princeton, NJ 08540

Just glue it!

Get lots of ideas for tree ornaments, kitchen accessories, and things to make and sell all year round. Request "Can Do Love Ideas from Elmer's" and "15 Ideas with Elmer's Glue in under 15 Minutes" from: Consumer Products Division, Borden, Inc., 180 E. Broad Street, Columbus, OH 43215

Further Resources for Teaching Kids Ages 9 to 12

The Kid's Money Book by Neale S. Godfrey, Checkerboard Press, 1991. For ages 8 and up, illustrated with color cartoon characters. Tells the story of how money began, how banks work, the stock market, and how to manage your own money. Written in a lighthearted question-and-answer format, the book answers hundreds of questions about money.

Money by Joe Cribb, Eyewitness Books Series, Alfred A. Knopf, Inc., 1990. For ages 8 and up. Outstanding color photography. Explores the symbolic and material meaning of money, from shekels, shells, and beads to gold, silver, checks, and credit cards. Pictures and names money from 20 foreign countries.

Kids' America by Steven Caney, Workman Publishing, 1979. Chapter 11 has excellent information on American coins, saving money, investing money, and going into business. Gives detailed plans for four business kids can run.

Fast Cash for Kids: 101 Money Making Projects for Young Entrepreneurs (2nd edition) by Bonnie and Noel Drew, Career Press, 1991. 101 inventive plans to take kids beyond the lemonade stand. Plus instructions on how to write a business plan, get customers, make a budget, advertise for free. Includes forms and worksheets to help kids get started.

Kids' Business Software, DiskCount Software, St. Paul, MN, 1990. Based on book *Fast Cash for Kids* by Bonnie and Noel Drew. This IBM software package provides 17 forms and worksheets, helps kids print a start-up manual, manages a database of customers, and prints business cards.

Making Cents: Every Kid's Guide to Money by Elizabeth Wilkinson, Little, Brown and Co., 1989. For ages 9 up, illustrated with wonderful pen and ink drawings and some photographs. All about what kids can do to have fun making money in their spare time. Short chapter on managing money.

Jobs for Kids: The Guide to Having Fun and Making Money by Carol Barkin and Elizabeth James, Lothrop, Lee & Shepard Books, 1990. For ages 10 and up, illustrated with cartoon drawings. How to select a job that's right for you, ideas on selling, setting prices, and getting customers, and a chapter on working for your parents.

Parentips: Quality Time with Kids by Bonnie Burgess Neely, Pocket Books, Simon & Schuster, Inc., 1987. Hundreds of low-cost, high-fun games for parents, grandparents, teachers, and baby-sitters to enjoy with kids of all ages. And lots of good, solid advice on raising kids.

Playing Smart: A Parent's Guide to Enriching, Offbeat Learning Activities for Ages 4-14 by Susan K. Perry, Free Spirit Publishing, 1990. Hundred's of ideas to enrich the time you spend with your child—from photography to psychology, cooking to cultural relativity.

It Doesn't Grow on Trees by Jean Ross Peterson, Betterway Publications, 1988. Practical advice on how to teach your child to be financially responsible. Addresses allowance, saving, work, investing, and healthy attitudes about money.

Bright Idea: Helps You Tackle Daily Life at Home by Dorothy Rich and Nancy Harter, The Home and School Institute, 1201 16th Street, NW, Washington, DC 20036, 1981. A cartoon workbook that helps families find better ways to solve problems in the home. Addresses positive communication with one another, organizing daily routines, and building good money habits.

1001 Things to Do With Your Kids by Caryl W. Krueger, Abingdon Press, 1988. Contains 1,001 ideas for things to do with your children from toddlers to teenagers. Designed to be done in the course of ordinary family events, making them more enjoyable and educational.

Chapter 5

Growing Up Responsible With Money

"I'm a great believer in luck, and I find the harder I work the more I have of it." —Thomas Jefferson

Give your child the advantage

Learning responsibility with money doesn't happen overnight. It develops gradually, day by day. It must be cultivated with patience, nurtured by parental supervision, and occasionally forced by allowing a child to experience the natural consequences of a poor decision.

Is it worth the investment of your time, energy, money, and resources? Without a doubt! Kids who are taught about money early have a great advantage in the game of life. They are equipped to be independent and armed with the money skills necessary for success. A solid financial education also teaches common sense, self-discipline, self-respect, and good work habits. The confidence your child develops will be carried into all areas of life, in school, at home, and in the community.

In order to reach the goal of teaching your child responsibility with money, you need a clear, well-defined and targeted list of steps to follow:

10 basic steps to teach kids responsibility with money

1. Examine your own attitudes about money.
2. Involve your child in family financial planning.
3. Give your child an allowance and let him be in charge of spending it.
4. Expect your child to contribute to family chores.
5. Provide extra income opportunities.
6. Teach your child to save regularly.
7. Help your child discover the satisfaction of sharing.
8. Show your child how to be a wise consumer.

9. Teach your child a healthy attitude toward credit.
10. Teach your child the value of wise investments.

This list actually summarizes the entire contents of **MoneySkills**. To keep your goals in sight, read the list frequently. Then evaluate what you have done in the last four weeks to make progress toward each step.

There will be times when you feel you've done well and times when you wonder if your child will ever stop being so irresponsible. That's normal. The rest of this chapter is devoted to identifying and addressing some of the money problems and questions you may encounter on your journey toward financial responsibility.

Allowance or the dole system: Which is better?

The dole system—giving kids money when they ask for it or when you think it is appropriate—gives your child only limited experience in handling money. You make all the decisions. The child feels like a beggar, and you resent constant requests for more money.

An allowance is the best way to teach your child about money. Most child development experts say every child over 5 should have an allowance. How much? The allowance should be large enough to give your child opportunities to make financial decisions, but small enough to discourage wastefulness.

Should kids do chores to earn allowance?

The experts say no. Kids who are paid for making their bed and taking out the trash (regular daily chores) are likely to develop the attitude they should be paid every time they pick up a sock.

Children should be taught to do chores because it is their contribution to the family and not to be paid. Your child's allowance is a share of the family income because "we love you." When the allowance is taken away because of poor performance, your child gets the message "we only love you when you are good." Allowances should never depend on the child's behavior, chores, or good grades.

What about an advance?

The time will come—sooner than you think—when your child will ask for his allowance early. "Look! They've got the race car I've been looking for, and there's only one left!" Now you are in a predicament. If you say "no" and the race car is gone on allowance day, your child will blame you for ruining everything because you are *so mean*. If you say "yes," you are a wonderful parent—who may have just started a child down the road to financial disaster.

Children must be taught early that we earn money or save money *before* we spend money. Advances on allowance say it's okay to spend money before you get it. That's instant gratification. It may not seem like much when you're dealing with a 5-year-old and a 50-cent allowance. But once the credit habit is introduced, it can grow into a terrible monster that follows your child throughout life.

Do yourself and your child a big favor. Say "no." Stick to your original plan. Stay calm. "I know you want the beautiful-race-car-that-everyone-else-has-and-you-don't. But allowance time is Wednesday, right after supper, at the kitchen table—not today and not here in the store." And remember, you must be faithful about giving the allowance at that time and place. Or your words will be challenged, you won't have any ground to stand on, and you will be pleaded with until you give in—not just this time, but again and again and again.

How do I know when to give my child a raise in allowance?

There has never been a kid who did *not* complain that his allowance is too small. Allowance reviews should be performed at least once every six months. *MoneySkill* 90 provides suggestions on how to handle the review. Most parents find it appropriate to give raises in allowance on a child's birthday or at the beginning of a new school year.

Should I give my child money for special occasions?

In general, the allowance is meant to cover small weekly expenses. Special occasions arise throughout the year when kids need more money: vacation, holidays, some big-ticket item your child wants to buy (a bicycle, a leather jacket, a sports car). Parents can approach these special occasions in two ways: 1) You can dip into your pocketbook and dish out the extra money; or 2) you can provide extra income opportunities for your child to supplement his weekly allowance. The danger of choosing the first option is that once you start dishing out extra money, you have undermined the whole allowance program and you will be forever trapped in a cycle of "dip and give."

Many parents have found that providing extra income opportunities is a successful method of handling occasions when the allowance is too small. Make a list of "above-and-beyond-the-call-of-duty" jobs your child can do around the house. Post your list in a place where young entrepreneurs can see it often.

Older children may also be encouraged to start their own business enterprises. Suggest that your child offer to do jobs for people in the neighborhood. Earning money for special jobs at home or for neighbors gives kids a greater sense of freedom and recognition than having money given to them for nothing.

What if my child is too shy to ask for a job?

Help your child by offering practical alternatives:

1. Let her work for you.
2. Tell friends and relatives your child wants to work. After she gets some work experience, she is not likely to feel so afraid.
3. Suggest that she get a partner. Kids often find it easier to speak to customers with a friend along to back them up.
4. Get customers to call her. Help your child make flyers and advertise that she is willing to work.

Fear is overcome by thinking about the positive (I'm going to earn some money) rather than the negative. (I'm afraid I'll be embarrassed when I talk to people.) Encourage your child to think about the rewards of working, what she can buy with the money, and how proud she will feel for taking initiative.

What if my child finds he can't do the job?

Your child will need your support if he gets in over his head by accepting a job he really can't do. Give him lots of encouragement. Send him back to try again. If he still can't do it right, go to your neighbor's house and help your child complete the job. If this is impossible, help your child make his apologies and get out of the situation gracefully. Most people are very understanding and realize when they hire a child these things can happen. Don't criticize your child at all! Help him learn from the experience and express your support for him in future efforts.

Should kids get paid for grades?

Children should not be paid to make grades. Children need to learn the value of doing their best because it makes them feel good, not because they are bribed.

There are many ways to reward your child for doing well for making a special effort. Verbal praise and recognition from parents is one of the best. If you want to give your child a gift, a special privilege, or a surprise, do so in a way that she does not construe the gift as pay for grades. Do not announce or offer the reward in advance.

Should parents ever loan kids money?

Credit is a fact of life in our society. Kids need to know how to use credit wisely and the dangers of credit abuse. Loans can be useful teaching tools when handled with care.

If you decide to loan your child money, set strict terms for repayment. The loan amount should not exceed one month's allowance. Make a complete written contract stating interest charges, a schedule of potential late fees, and/or collateral to be confiscated for nonpayment. When your child is late, impose the late fee or repossess your property.

You may find it a good plan to withhold a set amount from each allowance until the loan is paid, or post a list of extra chores your child can do to earn the money. Never allow your child to become entrapped in hopeless debt.

How can I get my child to save?

First consider your own saving habits. Your example either encourages or discourages saving. If saving is something you plan to do "someday," your child will likely view saving with an equal lack of interest.

Open a savings account for your child at a bank that has a savings "club" for kids. Consider offering to match what your child deposits for a period of time, dollar for dollar.

Help your child keep track of her savings with a chart. Display the chart where she can see it everyday and think about her goal.

Give your child reasons to save. If he wants a fancy bike or expensive clothes, let him save for it. When your child needs a boost toward a long-term goal, offer to buy something that compliments his purchase. (If he buys the bike, you'll buy the helmet.)

What's the worst mistake parents make with their kids and money?

Many parents get into financial trouble because they can't tell their children no. This can be dangerous both to the family's financial welfare and to the child's development.

It's tough when your kid's friend down the street seems to be able to afford anything and everything. Nevertheless, children need to understand there are limits and times when we have to say no to luxuries that are beyond the family budget.

Respect your own financial needs. Say no when your child's requests undermine the family financial picture. Do your best to give each child the same financial advantages. Set limits and enforce rules objectively and consistently. Kids appreciate authority when it is firm but fair.

How do you handle the problem of overspending?

Overspending is a habit that can't be reversed instantly. Trying suddenly to impose strict limits where none existed before will result in torture for both parents and child. It is best to approach the issue with the goal to gradually re-educate your child about spending:

1. Evaluate the kind of example *you* are setting.
2. Ask your child for suggestions to solve the problem.
3. Help your child deal with pressure from the media and peers. Talk about how TV commercials make us want to buy.
4. Have a family conference to discuss rules for allowances, handouts, and gifts. Explain how budgets work.
5. Ask relatives to limit gifts to special occasions.
6. Avoid stern lectures. Simply say, "I know you are disappointed, but it's not within our budget."
7. Let your child go without. Don't bail him out when he spends his allowance before the week is over.
8. Avoid making a habit of advancing allowance money. Kids get into the habit of spending money before they earn it.
9. If you make your child a personal loan, set up strict terms for repayment.
10. Some parents find temporarily revoking the allowance works for kids who refuse to listen to advice or warnings.
11. If reasonable measures such as those listed here fail, counseling may be necessary. Overspending is sometimes an effort to compensate for things we lack in life.

The key word for dealing with overspending is "accountability." It's a word we don't hear very often any more. But children need to learn they will be accountable for their financial decisions. No one can escape the consequences of their actions, and we must all accept responsibility for ourselves.

How can I talk to my child about peer pressure?

Ask your child what her favorite article of clothing is right now. Then ask, "Why do you like this outfit so much?" (Don't settle for vague answers like, "It's cool.") Is it the color? Is it because it's comfortable? Is it because you feel good when you wear this outfit? Does anyone you know have an outfit like this? Would you wear this outfit if your friends didn't like it?

This can easily lead into a talk about peer pressure and other issues such as drugs, alcohol, and sex and the importance of using your own good judgement. Keep the discussion friendly and non-threatening. You may be surprised at the honest communication that develops if your child feels safe to be herself with you.

Here's something else you can talk about. Adults don't call it peer pressure, but we know it's necessary to dress at least as well as everyone else at the office or workplace. Is all peer pressure bad?

What are some of kids' most common money problems?

1. **Blowing money on fads.** Don't preach. An allowance is for discretionary spending, so let your child learn on his own.
2. **Wastefulness around the house.** Enlist the family in efforts to control waste. Set guidelines together. Then assess fines for infractions and give rewards for improvements.
3. **"Just write a check."** Take kids to the bank and let them see you deposit a paycheck. Let them see you pay the bills and buy groceries.
4. **Borrowing.** Demonstrate responsibility with credit by insisting IOU's be paid. If you borrow from the kids, pay back on time and with interest.
5. **Credit-*itis*.** Explain that it's expensive to "rent" someone else's money. Charge interest even on small loans.
6. **Running over budget.** Help set up a plan for weekly spending. Let a child age 11 or 12 suffer the consequences of decisions. If necessary, give the allowance daily for a while. Require your child to keep a money diary.
7. **Losing money.** Be sure your child has a safe way to carry money. Only replace money needed for essentials, like lunch money or bus fare.
8. **Expecting to be paid for half-hearted effort on jobs.** Set standards that must be met before getting paid.
9. **Inability to save.** Require that 10 percent of the allowance go into savings immediately. Add "found money" to savings. Help your child experience the satisfaction of saving.

10. Requesting inappropriate purchases. Don't use money as an excuse to say no about something you don't want your kid to do. Tell the real reason: the product is not appropriate, you don't approve of the requested privilege, or the child is not mature enough for this new responsibility.

What about the problem of begging?

Once a child gets what he wants by begging, he will use that strategy again and again. "She doesn't really mean no. If I fuss a little harder, she'll change her mind." I don't think any parent consciously decides to sentence themselves to 18 years of hassle and arguments. Nevertheless, "begging 'til you give in" is a strategy your child will employ with ever-increasing skill until the day he leaves home—and maybe even longer—if he finds it successful.

Establishing a set of ground rules about money, shopping, the family budget, loans, and allowances is the best deterrent to begging. Ground rules help prevent us from being embarrassed and harassed by our begging children. Ground rules also teach children important lessons:

- The value of planning ahead
- Patience
- Politeness and respect for others
- Self-discipline
- To delay gratification

Of course, every child will test the limits you set. Stick firmly with the ground rules. If you make a practice of giving in when a child begs, he or she learns that begging is an acceptable way to get what you want. That, of course, is not what we mean to teach.

Why do kids want everything they see on TV?

In one morning of watching TV, your child may see up to $3,000 worth of products advertised. No wonder kids ask for so many things! What can you do?

1. Set limits. Tell your child how much you will spend or how many presents she should expect on birthdays or holidays.
2. Think how your child feels. Tell her, "I can see why you want that new toy. It looks like fun on TV." Then explain why you won't buy it.
3. Listen to your child's unspoken needs: love, time with you, to know she is first and most important. Kids don't know how to say these things, but they see commercials with everyone happy and loving each other and they want to feel that way, too. Give your child a hug!

How do you deal with a child who loses his allowance?

The first time your child loses money, replace it. Calmly discuss how the money got lost and what your child might do to avoid losing his money from now on. Help him find a safe place to carry money and a safe place to keep money at home. Explain that next time, you will not replace the money and he will have to do without until the next allowance day. Do not threaten or lecture. Just explain the facts calmly.

The second time, let your child suffer the natural consequences of his actions. It may hurt you worse than it hurts him, but let him do without. He will learn by experience that there are consequences to being careless. If this is an older child who needs the money for school or bus, you may need to let him borrow from next week's allowance. Make a written contract or IOU and post it on the refrigerator or kitchen bulletin board. Next week on allowance day, take the money to pay his IOU out of his allowance and give him the remainder.

If a child continues to lose money, more drastic measures will be required: 1) Let him earn the money he needs for the week; 2) Let him borrow, but charge him interest; or 3) keep his money for him for the next four weeks. Explain that he will continue to receive the same allowance, but you will keep it for him in a safe place. Give him a small notebook to write down how much he has spent each day and to keep account of how much is left. Give him the money only as he needs it. Tell him you are showing him how to keep better account of his money and that by next month you feel sure he will be ready to handle his money more carefully. Continue to remain objective. Your goal is to teach your child to manage his own money. This won't happen if you cloud the issues with anger or guilt.

How do I teach my child not to be selfish?

Selfishness can become a lifelong habit pattern if not dealt with while your child is young.

1. First, look at your own life and see what kind of behavior you are modeling. Be sure you are not giving your child the message that happiness comes from material things.
2. Teach your child to share from the time she first gets an allowance. Use three banks to divide allowance money between Saving, Sharing, and Spending. (See Activities 23 and 52.) Then let your child help decide when and how her Sharing money is given.
3. Demonstrate generosity with time and resources. Make charity and volunteering a regular part of your family life.
4. Give your child opportunities to learn to enjoy sharing at home: buying treats for the family, contributing to family projects, buying small gifts for family members on birthdays or special occasions, taking friends to movies, buying gifts for birthday parties, etc.
5. Limit the number of presents you give your child for birthday and holidays. Children who get too much and are constantly coddled start thinking they deserve it all the time. Never give your child all that she asks for—even if you can afford it.
6. Take your child to visit a place where people are in need. Plan a visit to a veterans' home, a mission, or a shelter for the homeless. You won't have to preach any sermons. When children see people suffering and hungry, they are moved with compassion. Let your child

discover the satisfaction of sharing with those less fortunate. I guarantee she'll return home with a new attitude about material things.

What if my child steals money?

Asking "why" only invites the child to make excuses or stories to cover himself. The best way to deal with stealing is with action—quickly and firmly:

1. Require that your child return the item he stole and apologize in person.
2. Take away some of your child's privileges for a period of time.
3. If your child is caught stealing at school, support the disciplinary actions the school requires.
4. If stealing persists, professional therapy may be necessary. Sometimes stealing reflects a child's desire for revenge or feelings of very low self-esteem. Stealing can also be a sign that a child feels cheated by life and the world "owes" him something.

What about shoplifting?

It takes more than lectures to deter shoplifting and stealing. Here are some actions steps to take:

1. Guide your child into more supervised activities. Don't let your child hang out at stores because he has nothing better to do.
2. Closely supervise your child when you are at the store together.
3. Monitor and restrict time with friends that may be tempting him to shoplift.
4. Take away privileges until your child shows he is mature enough to be trusted.
5. Talk to your child about the dangers of even being seen with someone who shoplifts. Explain what a serious offense this is, and what happens to people who are caught shoplifting.
6. It's sad to say, but getting caught is the best thing that can happen to a child. Most kids are so scared and embarrassed by their experience with the police that taking things loses all its glamour.

How do I explain to my child if I lose my job?

Small children are affected by offhand statements parents make about money. ("I don't know how we'll pay all the bills this month.") They are tremendously affected and insecure when major financial difficulties arise. Children may feel profound grief as the realities of job loss ripple through the family.

Call a family conference to talk with your children honestly about the situation. Explain that every human being has times when things go wrong. This is not fun, but it is an opportunity for your family to learn how to work together to solve problems. Talk about other times in your life when you've made it through difficult situations. Maintain a sense of hope. Show your child how to be persistent. Teach your child that people are special because of who they are, not what jobs they have.

How can children be involved in family financial planning?

Invite your child to participate in a family planning conference. Meetings should be short, particularly if the children are young. Thirty minutes is a long time to a child in grade school. Try not to make it too boring. Include talk about good things that have happened that week, progress on plans for vacation, and decisions that need to be made about money. Occasionally let the kids be in charge of the meeting. You may learn a lot about your children by watching how they handle the family meeting.

What do children learn from family planning conferences?

1. We have to have money to operate the household
2. We must plan how we *get* money and how we *use* money.
3. Money has to be earned. It doesn't appear by magic.
4. The family can help money go further by doing things ourselves.
5. When there is not enough money to cover everything we want, we have to make choices.
6. Monthly bills like rent, house payments, and utilities must be paid first.
7. Allowances have to fit in with the family budget.
8. When one expense increases, another must decrease.
9. The objective is to keep expenses even with or less than income.
10. It's important to have a financial plan.

Family planning conferences are not for the purpose of burdening kids or making them worry about finances. The purpose is solely to educate them about the mechanics of running the household and the limits of the family budget.

Kids who are involved in helping make the decisions are less likely to feel like helpless victims or "nobodies" whose opinions don't count. They are less likely to resent limits.

What kind of ground rules should we establish?

Many parents don't have financial planning sessions with their kids because they are afraid kids will tell the neighbors how much they earn. Don't use this for an excuse. It isn't necessary to reveal your total income to the children in order for them to be included in a family financial meeting.

Avoid other problems by setting up some ground rules:

- How each person may participate
- The importance of confidentiality
- How often sessions will be held, as well as when and where
- Research members need to do ahead of time on major purchases

- What decisions the family planning session will make and what decisions parents will reserve for themselves
- The importance of listening to each family member
- Time to discuss both short-term and long-term family financial goals

What's a good way to discuss the budget?

Make a giant pie chart on a piece of posterboard to show how your paycheck is used to pay bills and run the household. Explain how a portion of the family income goes to pay for the house, the telephone, the electricity, the water, groceries, doctors, clothes, taxes, recreation, etc.

Your attitude should communicate that the budget is serious, but not frightening, and that Mom & Dad are in control. Show kids how you make budget cuts and adjustments when they are needed, making some pieces of the pie smaller for a while. Then show them how you enlarge parts of the pie when you have extra money.

What other things should we talk about?

Discuss ways you can earn or save money together for special goals. Jean Ross Peterson (*It Doesn't Grow on Trees*, Betterway Publications) tells the story of one family who formed an allowance pool. The children wanted a VCR, but the family didn't have the money in the budget. So they had a family planning conference and hatched a plan. They agree to save together for the VCR. Each week the parents put in $5 and the kids put in $1 until there was enough money in the allowance pool for the VCR. The plan worked so well that the family now uses the allowance pool to save for vacations, to buy stock, and other special projects. By working together and keep-ing goals clear, your whole family can learn valuable lessons about saving.

One Important Word: Communication

As you implement the activities recommended in this book, you will have many opportunities for meaningful communication with your child. Sometimes you will talk about money. Other times you may talk about school, pets, baseball, first jobs, the future, what it was like when you were a kid, or outer space. *What* you talk about is not as important as *how* you communicate. If your talk is mostly a lecture or sermon, your child will tune you out. If you really want to communicate with a child, you must be honest and share from the heart. You must never talk down to a child and you must have a genuine desire to know your child. In practical application, that means talking about what your child is interested in. Here are some suggestions:

1. Everyone has to do something for the first time. For a child, this can be scary. Tell your child about the first job you ever had or the first time you ever got paid for doing work. How old were you? How did you get the job? What was it like? How did you feel? How did you spend the money?

2. Tell a funny story about a time you bought something you thought was a real bargain, but it turned out to be a "lemon." What made you think you were getting a good deal? Where did you get the money? How did you feel when you discovered you had bought a lemon? What did you do about it?

3. Start a discussion by sharing a story about a time when you bought something or wore something just because everyone else was doing it. How did you happen to get into that situation? Were you pleased with your decision? How did it turn out?

4. Tell your child about something you wanted and saved for when you were a kid. Why did you want that item so badly? What did you do to get the money? How did you feel when you finally had enough money to buy it?

173

The rewards

In the first chapter of *MoneySkills,* we talked about an important question: What do you want your child to learn about money? It's not a question many parents find easy to answer. But after reading this book, I'm sure you have a much better idea—and perhaps even a definite list—of the money attitudes, values, facts, skills, and habits with which you want to equip your child.

As you continue to use the activities and fine-tune the principles you've learned in *MoneySkills*, remember that no one is a perfect parent who is able to prepare their child for every circumstance. Give yourself room for mistakes and give your child permission to be what he or she is—a child who is learning, growing, and developing. All of your goals won't be accomplished in one afternoon or even in several afternoons. It will take days, months, and even years of consistent practice and patient guidance to prepare your child for the future. But I'm sure you agree that the ultimate reward of seeing your son or daughter step confidently into adulthood—prepared, financially responsible, and independent—will make it worth every minute you've invested.

Send your ideas

If you have ideas, suggestions, or comments about kids and money to share with the author, please write. Any information or personal stories you send will be extremely helpful in our research for the next book.

Bonnie Drew
MoneySkills
c/o Career Press
P.O. Box 34
Hawthorne, NJ 07507

Additional Activities Forms

Included in this section are additional copies of various forms, worksheets and samples found in the MoneySkills activities throughout the book. You may use them to make photocopies or simply cut them out of the book.

Found in Chapter 1

Financial Facts of Life

1. Attitudes—What feelings or emotions about money do you want to pass along to the next generation? Example: generosity.

2. Values—What code of money ethics do you want your child to live by? Examples: honesty, family and health come before money.

3. Facts—What basic knowledge about money will be necessary for your child to function properly in society? Examples: How credit cards work; what savings bonds are.

4. Skills—What must your child be competent to do with money? Examples: making change, developing a weekly budget.

5. Habits—What regular financial practices should be a part of your child's life? Examples: saving, goal setting.

Found in Activity 2

penny

nickel

dime

quarter

Found in Activity 19

TODAY'S DATE

TINY TOT BANK
1901 SMITH ST.
ANYTOWN, U.S.A.

PAY TO THE
ORDER OF

TEN DOLLARS AND 00 CENT   **$ 10.00**

AMOUNT

YOUR NAME

TODAY'S DATE

TINY TOT BANK
1901 SMITH ST.
ANYTOWN, U.S.A.

PAY TO THE
ORDER OF

TEN DOLLARS AND 00 CENT   **$ 10.00**

AMOUNT

YOUR NAME

TODAY'S DATE

TINY TOT BANK
1901 SMITH ST.
ANYTOWN, U.S.A.

PAY TO THE
ORDER OF

TWENTY DOLLARS AND 00 CENT   **$ 20.00**

AMOUNT

YOUR NAME

Found in Activity 50

In Honor of Your Birthday

Name: _____

Age: _____

Date: _____

We're proud of you because:

Your new privileges this year are:

Your special responsibilities will be:

It's going to be a great year!

Signed: _____ (Parents)

_____ (Child)

Found in Activity 54

MY CHECK REGISTER

Check #	Date	Paid To	Amount	Balance

Found in Activity 69

PRICE TRACKING CHART
(ITEM:) _____

Week #	Date	Price	Difference

Found in Activity 72

PRODUCT SURVEY

Question:

Product #1:   **Product #2:**

Record answers to your survey by coloring one block for each vote on the correct bar graph.

Results: _____

Found in Activity 87

Credit Application

Name: _____   Age: _____

Address: _____

Phone: _____   School: _____

Sources of income: Money you owe:
1.   1.

2.   2.

3.   3.

People who have loaned you money before:

1.

2.

Amount you wish to borrow: _____

What the money will be used for:_____
_____

Your plans for repaying the loan:_____
_____

Date loan will be paid:_____

Approved   ❑

Not approved   ❑

Borrower: _____

Loan officer: _____

Found in Activity 91

MY SPENDING PLAN

	Week 1		Week 2	
	Planned	Spent	Planned	Spent
Fixed Expenses:				
Flexible Expenses:				
Totals:				

Use this chart to see how well you stayed on your spending plan.

Activity Index

MoneySkills